Fashion Footwear

1800-1970

Schiffer Publishing Ltd

4880 Lower Valley Road, Atglen, PA 19310 USA

Desire Smith

Designed by "Sue"
Type set in Windsor BT bolded/Souvenir Lt BT

ISBN: 0-7643-1132-8
Printed in China
1 2 3 4

Published by Schiffer Publishing Ltd.
4880 Lower Valley Road
Atglen, PA 19310
Phone: (610) 593-1777; Fax: (610) 593-2002
E-mail: Schifferbk@aol.com
Please visit our web site catalog at **www.schifferbooks.com**
We are always looking for people to write books on new and related subjects. If you have an idea for a book, please contact us at the above address.

This book may be purchased from the publisher.
Include $3.95 for shipping. Please try your bookstore first.
You may write for a free catalog.

In Europe, Schiffer books are distributed by
Bushwood Books
6 Marksbury Ave. Kew Gardens
Surrey TW9 4JF England
Phone: 44 (0)208-392-8585; Fax: 44 (0)208-392-9876
E-mail: Bushwd@aol.com
Free postage in the UK. Europe: air mail at cost.
Please try your bookstore first.

This book is

affectionally dedicated

to my sons

Matthew Boyd Smith

and

Michael Wagner Smith

Men's 1970s black leather platform oxfords, with a "city-landscape" painted on the heels. *Courtesy of Matthew Smith.*

Acknowledgments

My husband, Bruce Smith, who gained his facility with the language long before there was a "spell check," has given me countless hours of critical analysis, which has been invaluable. My son Matthew has added substantially to my shoe collection with his wonderful "finds," and my son Michael has added substantially to my knowledge of the computer and been my "troubleshooter" whenever I needed help. There is a warm place in my heart for our family dogs, Honey and Bullit, who have worked with me long hours at the computer and in my photography studio, giving their loyalty and companionship.

I also thank the models who give life to the book. They worked with me to make each photograph special, taking time from their busy schedules and even giving up their days off. In alphabetical order, the models are: Marcie Behanna, Colleen Bergin, Elisa Buratto, Emily Fischer, Bridget Foy, Adria Hadley, Francesca Stewart, Tess Stewart, and Jennifer Weigand.

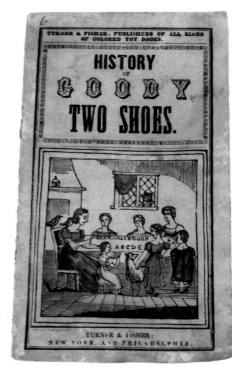

Opposite page photo:
Strapless couture gown of ivory net, decorated with hand applied iridescent sequins and clear rhinestones. Worn with 1950s clear plastics slingback sandals with Lucite heels. *Modeled by Marcie Behanna photographed by the author.*

Original copy of *History of Goody Two Shoes*, published by Turner & Fisher, New York and Philadelphia, 1838. *Courtesy of Bruce Smith.*

Karen Augusta (of North Westminster, Vermont, and www.antique-fashion.com), an important dealer in antique clothing, trusted me with some exquisite shoes from her stock, enhancing the work immeasurably. Liz McGarrity, New York artist and costume designer, not only permitted me to photograph some fascinating shoes from her collection, but spent many hours interviewing Howard Davis, shoe designer and instructor at Parsons School of Design, making it possible for me to include this priceless interview here. I am deeply indebted to both Liz and Howard for their contributions.

Mary Efron (of Mary Efron, New York City), who has an unerring eye for fashion, permitted me to photograph a number of shoes from her stock. Renee Weiss Chase, Head of the Fashion Design Program at the Nesbitt College of Design Arts at Drexel University, and Bella Veksler, curator of the Drexel University Historical Costume Collection (cited as DUHCC in the captions), permitted me to photograph many shoes from the collection, including rare examples by Salvatore Ferragamo and other important designers. These shoes added substantially to the book and I am very grateful.

David Sterner, an antiques dealer and our nephew, contributed several wonderful pairs of shoes to my collection, and I am very thankful.

I am also thankful to my friends and associates in fashion for help and guidance: Louise Stewart, fashion designer and "stage mother," generously helped style the photographic "shoots" with her daughter, Tess. Maryjanet McNamara, fashion designer, designed the red slip dress worn by Francesca Stewart. My friends Barbara Consorto and Angela Grimes gave moral support and critical help with photography and the computer. Lisa Leaverton, costume designer and stylist, permitted me to photograph her "Campbell's Souper Dress," provided the tiara, and helped style the "Cinderella shoot" with Elisa Buratto. Patty Fischer let me photograph a wonderful pair of wedge-heeled slippers from the estate of Elizabeth P. Fischer. I am indebted to Joyce Ruth, Kim Hemingway, and the Sanford A. Alderfer Auction Company of Hatfield, Pennsylvania, for permitting me to photograph the 1860s ice skates. Finally, special thanks to Donna Sigler, my friend and art teacher many years ago at Solebury School, for ferreting out some great shoes for my collection.

Thanks to the many dealers and auctioneers who sold me shoes over the years. I hope the shoes have found a home in this book. Finally, to Nancy Schiffer, my editor, and to Sue Taylor, the talented designer who put the book together, my sincere thanks.

Contents

Introduction

Burgundy leather and suede high shoes or boots, with front laces and a Louis XV heel, 1890-1900.

Fashion Footwear: 1800-1970, is a handbook for collectors, shoe designers, costume designers, antique and vintage clothing consultants and dealers, and anyone who just loves shoes! The book divides footwear, which includes shoes, boots, and sandals, into two major categories: Antique Footwear, pre-1940, and Vintage Footwear, 1940-1970. There is no clear consensus among clothing dealers and collectors as to what should be considered "antique" and what should be considered "vintage." The current thinking expressed in the words of one important dealer is that "if cars can be considered antiques at fifty years, why not something as ephemeral as clothing?"

The book is a picture book, with several important additions. *Fashion Footwear* includes an interview of a shoe designer, which gives us an understanding of the craft of the shoe, and a *Footwear Glossary,* which gives us an understanding of shoe related terminology. Each item of footwear is described in detail, identified as to style, age, material, designer or brand, and store name if given. Heel types and heights are carefully measured and recorded in the descriptions. Price ranges reflect the current market retail prices, but are subject to regional differences. Highest prices are always paid for shoes in excellent condition, in unusual colors, and unique styles.

The majority of the shoes pictured are from the author's collection, but *Fashion Footwear* includes important additions from private collections and from Drexel University's Historical Costume Collection. Photographs generally include both shoes, because shoes are designed as a pair. Some of the vintage shoes are worn by models, as part of a complete fashion ensemble.

Names of manufacturers, retailers and designers are recorded as they are printed on the insoles of the shoes, which accounts for the somewhat unusual use of capital and lower case letters in descriptive material and in the corresponding index entries.

Pale green brocade slingback wedge-soled slipper, with decorative perforations on the vamp, and silver kid detailing, 1930s. *Courtesy of the Estate of Elizabeth P. Fischer.*

Iridescent purple leather high shoe or boot, with side buttons and a Louis XV heel, 1890-1900. *Courtesy of DUHCC.*

Black suede T-strap evening sandal, 1930s. *Courtesy of DUHCC.*

Black suede ankle-strap platform sandal, with a Cuban heel, 1940s.

Rust suede open-toed slingback platform pump, with brown leather floral decoration on the vamp, and a boulevard heel, 1940s. *Courtesy of DUHCC*.

Brown alligator pump with a boulevard heel, 1940s.

Pale blue leather and suede open-shank pump, with perforations on the vamp, and a stiletto heel, 1950s.

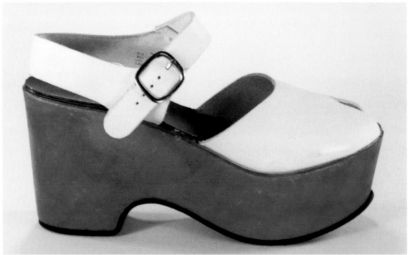

White leather open-toed, ankle-strap platform sandal, with a Dutch boy heel, 1970s.

Antique Footwear

Early 1800s

It is very rare to find 18th century footwear for sale. The best sources of information about these shoes and boots are books about the history of costume.

Although it is not easy, it is possible to find early 19th century shoes. Shoes worn for work or everyday are almost nonexistent. Made of heavy leather, often without a tongue, (strip of leather inside the throat of a shoe, usually under lace or buckle), these shoes were very often worn out and thrown away. If you do find such a pair, it is difficult to ascertain age, unless provenance and family history is available. Stylistic dating is impossible with such shoes that have no particular style.

Tucked away in a blanket chest with a favorite gown, were the kid and silk slippers. Similar in appearance to our contemporary ballet flats, these fragile, early nineteenth century shoes are likely to be made of silk, and lined with either cotton twill or linen. Sometimes adorned with a silk rosette or bow, or a metal buckle, these shoes are lightweight and collapsible, their soles paper-thin. We might catch sight of a pair of these slippers at an antique show, carefully placed in a glass display case. The dealer who offers the shoes may believe that they are from the eighteenth century, because the left and right soles are indistinguishable. The soles are "straight" and fit either foot.

The early nineteenth century slippers can be found in pastel colors, but are most commonly made of ivory silk, or ivory kid. I have seen them in black kid and black silk, also. The style is unmistakable.

White kid slipper, lined with ivory homespun linen; pointed toe and tan leather straight sole, slightly thicker at the heel; American, 1780-1790. *Courtesy of Karen Augusta.* $475-525.

Straight sole of white kid slipper. Notice the pointed toe, which is characteristic of the period.

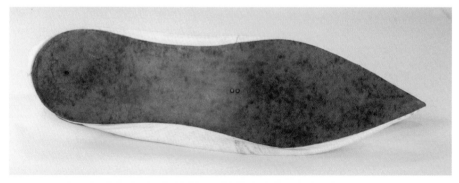

1820s

As the century progresses, the shoes become heavier. The stacked heel, made of layers of leather, is common by the mid-nineteenth century.

Ivory silk slipper, lined with ivory cotton twill, with a silk ribbon tie; thin tan leather straight sole, 1820-1830. *Courtesy of DUHCC.* $250-275.

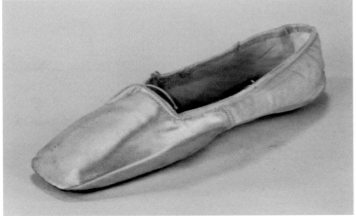

Ivory silk slipper with pull string, lined with ivory cotton twill; thin tan leather straight sole, 1820-1830. *Courtesy of DUHCC.* $250-275 pair.

Mauve silk slipper with pull string, lined with ivory linen and kid; thin tan leather straight sole, 1820-1830. *Courtesy of DUHCC.* $250-275 pair.

Showing the thin tan leather straight sole of the mauve silk slipper, 1820-1830. *Courtesy of DUHCC.*

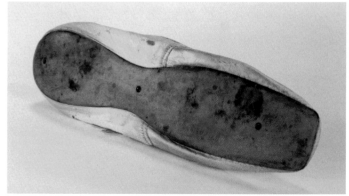

1830s

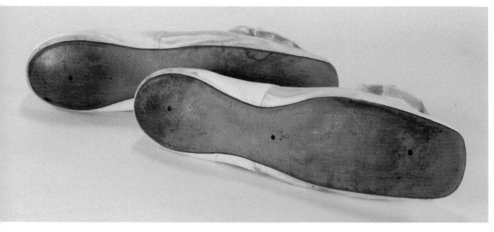

Above left:
Black silk slipper with silk bows, lined with ivory cotton twill; thin tan leather straight sole, 1830-1840. *Courtesy of DUHCC.* $275-325.
Above:
Ivory silk slipper with elaborate silk bows, edged in lace, lined with ivory cotton twill; thin tan leather straight sole, 1830-1840. *Courtesy of DUHCC.* $275-325.
Left:
Showing the thin tan leather soles of the ivory silk slippers, 1830-1840. *Notice that the soles are straight, not crooked. Courtesy of DUHCC.*

In terms of the marketplace, the most valuable shoes are the elaborately beaded shoes and boots of the late 19th and early 20th century. Some of these are made of iridescent kid, in such stunning shades as gold and burgundy. Collectors also prize the two-tone, suede and leather shoes, in subtle pastel colors.

1840s

Purple silk dainty boot, with side laces, and tan leather straight sole with a square toe, lined with ivory linen, 1840-1845. *Courtesy of DUHCC.* $375-425.

Tan cotton dainty boot, with side laces and brown leather heel cap; tan leather straight sole, lined with ivory cotton twill, 1845-1850. *Courtesy of Karen Augusta.* $300-350.

Tan cotton dainty boot, showing side laces.

Tan silk dainty boot, with side laces, and tan leather straight sole, lined with ivory linen. 1840-1845. *Courtesy of DUHCC.* $300-350.

Black silk dainty boot, with side laces and ties; tan leather straight sole with 1-inch stacked heel; lined with ivory linen. 1845-1850. *Courtesy of DUHCC.* $325-375.

Rust silk dainty boot, with side laces and ties; tan leather straight sole with 1-inch stacked heel; lined with ivory linen. 1845-1850. *Courtesy of DUHCC.* $325-375.

1850s

By 1850 shoes become "crooked," showing a distinction between left and right.

Brown kid low shoe with a solid gold buckle on the vamp, and pleated brown silk under the buckle and across the instep, lined with ivory kid; straight sole with 2-1/2-inch leather covered heel. 1850-1855. $375-425.

Brown leather high shoe or boot, side-buttoned with 13 glass buttons, scalloped at top and around button closures; lined with ivory cotton twill; tan leather straight sole with 1-inch stacked heel. 1850-1860. *Courtesy of Karen Augusta.* $350-425.

1860s

The "Louis" heel (having a curved outline, flared at base) and the "baby Louis" heel (like the "Louis" in shape, but lower) appear, and by 1870 the high-button shoe, or boot, is in fashion. Often the tops of these shoes are scalloped (curving or circular segments, forming an ornamental edge), or a pinking tool is used to decorate the leather (by adding a saw tooth edge to the scalloping).

Black kid high shoe or boot, with open laces fastened with 9 glass buttons; ivory kid lining; brown leather straight sole with 2-inch Louis XV leather covered heel, 1865-1870. *Courtesy of DUHCC.* $425-475.

Black high shoe showing the open laces in detail.

Ice skates, with steel blades and leather straps,
imprinted on bottom of the skates, "Bushnell & Tull,
Philada," 1860-1865. *Courtesy of Sanford A.
Alderfer Auction Company.* $475-525.

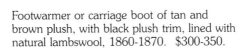

Footwarmer or carriage boot of tan and
brown plush, with black plush trim, lined with
natural lambswool, 1860-1870. $300-350.

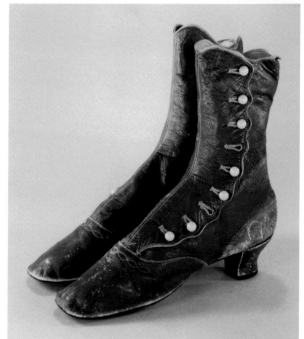

Black silk velvet low shoe, with eyelets and laces over instep; lined with ivory silk; tan leather slightly crooked sole with 1-1/2-inch black silk velvet covered heel. 1875-1880. *Courtesy of DUHCC.* $400-450.

Cornflower blue kid high shoe or boot with decorative stitching on vamp, scalloped at the top and around button closures; side fastened with 9 white iridescent glass buttons; lined with ivory kid; slightly crooked tan leather sole with a 1-1/2 Louis XV heel, covered with blue kid, 1870-1880. $675-725.

Black silk velvet slipper, satin embroidered on the vamp in shades of green, burgundy, and blue; lined with ivory kid and ivory cotton twill; tan leather slightly crooked sole with 1-1/4-inch stacked heel, 1875-1880. *Courtesy of Karen Augusta.* $325-375.

Silk velvet slipper showing the stacked heel.

Brown iridescent leather high shoe or boot, elaborately beaded on the front in a floral pattern with diminutive copper glass beads; scalloped side closure with eleven buttons; brown leather slightly crooked sole with a 1-1/2-inch stacked heel; lined with ivory cotton twill and bright blue silk satin, which is woven in gold on both shoes, "J. & J. SLATER, 1185 BROADWAY, N. Y.," 1875-1880. *Courtesy of Karen Augusta.* $675-725.

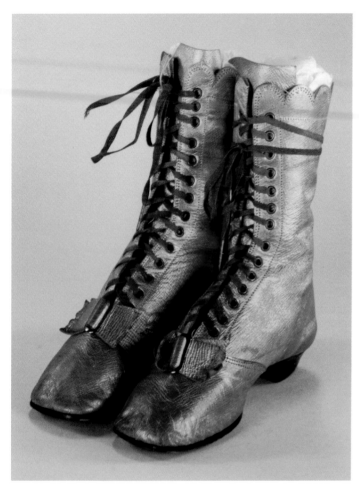

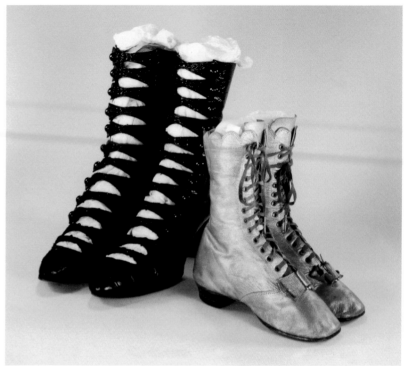

Showing the diminutive size of the child's gold leather high shoes.

Child's gold leather high shoe or boot, with a scalloped top, decorative gold leather bow, diminutive buckle, and front laces; 6-inch long slightly crooked tan leather sole with a 1-inch stacked heel; sole imprinted, "DUNBAR & Co., PHILA.," 1870-1880. *Courtesy of Karen Augusta.* $925-1000.

1880s

Lace-up styles become popular in the 1880s, and continue into the early decades of the 20th century. Generally speaking, the lace-up shoes, or boots, tend to be higher than the button-up shoes. Perhaps this is because the laces can be drawn tighter, affording more support for the high top. Contemporary thinking is that boots are distinguished from shoes by their height, over the ankle. When we carefully inspect the high shoes, or boots, we see that although these shoes reach above the ankle, they are no more sturdy in construction than the low pumps of the period.

Wooden roller skates, with wooden wheels, and leather straps, several patent dates are listed, including March 1882. *Courtesy of Karen Augusta.* $375-425.

Brown kid high shoe or boot, side buttoned with 11 glass buttons; scalloped at top and around button closures; lined with gold silk and ivory cotton twill; tan leather slightly crooked sole with 1-1/2-inch baby Louis heel. 1880-1885. $350-375.

27

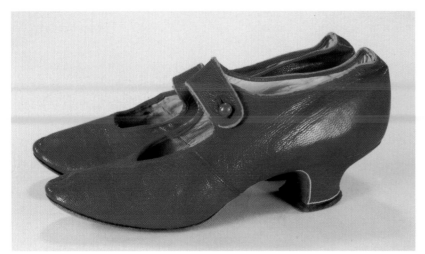

Red leather low shoe with a single strap over the instep, fastened with a red glass button; lined with ivory kid; insoles are stamped "Steigerwalt, Phila.:" crooked tan leather sole, with a 1-1/2-inch Louis XV red leather covered heel, 1880-1890. *Courtesy of DUHCC.* $350-375.

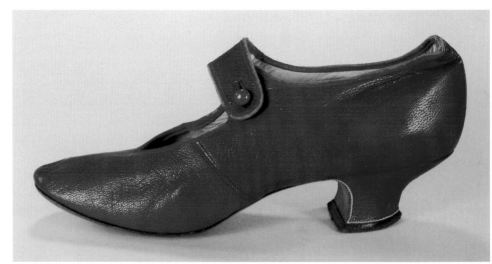

The red leather low shoe showing the leather covered heel, with stitching.

Gold kid low shoe with a single strap over the instep, fastened with a gold button; lined with ivory kid; crooked tan leather sole with 1-1/2-inch Louis XV heel, covered with gold kid. $375-425.

Showing the back of the gold kid low shoe, showing the flare at the base of the Louis XV heel.

Black faille carriage boot, with black faille ribbon ties and brown fur trim; lined with quilted silk satin; black leather crooked sole with a 1-inch molded heel, 1880-1885 *Courtesy of DUHCC.* $325-375.

Black velvet carriage boot, with black faille ribbon ties and brown fur trim; lined with quilted silk satin; black leather crooked sole with a 1-inch molded heel, 1880-1885. *Courtesy of DUHCC.* $325-375.

Purple iridescent leather high shoe or boot, side fastened with *eighteen* buttons; lined with ivory cotton twill, and signed on lining, "Madam Cheerie 3337;" crooked brown leather sole with 2-1/2-inch stacked heel, 1885-1890. *Courtesy of Karen Augusta.* $375-400.

1890s

Left:
Purple iridescent kid high shoe or boot, elaborately decorated on the vamp and straps over toes in amber glass stones and diminutive copper glass beads; additionally decorated on the ten straps which button on the side; lined with tan kid; Gold stamped on insole, "Cammey, Fifth Ave., N.Y.," crooked tan leather sole with 3-inch Louis XV heel, 1890-1900. *Purchased by the author from the Estate of Bertha K. Hershey.* $850-925.

Right:
The purple iridescent kid high shoes, showing the elaborately beaded straps.

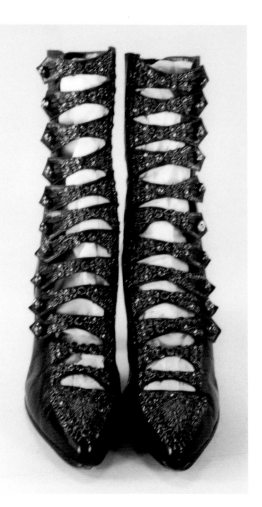

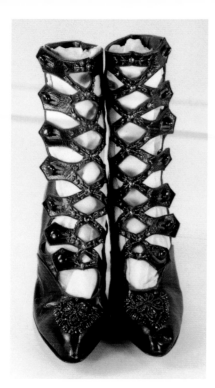

Far left:
Purple iridescent kid high shoe or boot, elaborately beaded on the vamp with copper glass beads; additionally decorated with copper glass beads on the seven straps which button on the side; lined with tan kid, and stamped on the insole, "N. Snellenburg & Co., Philadelphia, PA;" crooked tan leather sole with a 3-inch Louis XV heel, c. 1890-1900. $850-925.

Left:
The purple iridescent kid high shoes, showing the Louis XV heel.

Right:
Black leather carriage boot, trimmed with brown fur, and tied with black silk grosgrain ribbon; lined with ivory quilted satin, with woven label in right shoe, "Daniel Green;" black leather sole with molded heel, 1890-1900. $325-375.

The period between 1901 and 1910 is often called the Edwardian Era after Queen Victoria's successor, King Edward VII. Sophisticates of the day also referred to this time as the Belle Epoque, or "Beautiful Age."

1900s

The purple iridescent kid high shoes, showing the Louis XV heel.

Left:
Purple iridescent kid high shoe or boot, side fastened with 13 black glass buttons; ivory cotton twill lining, with kid at top of shoe; insole stamped, "I. MILLER, 1 West 42nd ST., NEW YORK:" brown leather crooked sole with 2-1/2-inch Louis XV heel, 1900-1910. *Courtesy of DUHCC.* $375-400.

Black leather high button shoe, or boot; side fastened with ten straps, elaborately beaded with black glass beads, and closed with black glass buttons; lined with black kidskin; crooked black leather sole, with a 2-1/2-inch heel; stamped in silver on the insole, "Strawbridge & Clothier, Philadelphia," 1905-1910. *Courtesy of Karen Augusta.* $625-700.

Brown suede high shoe or boot, with decorative perforations and stitching on the vamp, and fastened on the side with 14 buttons; lined with ivory cotton twill and kid; gold stamped on both boots on lining near top, "Walk Over Trade Mark Reg. U. S. PAT. OFF.," brown leather sole with 2-inch stacked heel, 1905-1915. *Courtesy of DUHCC.* $325-375.

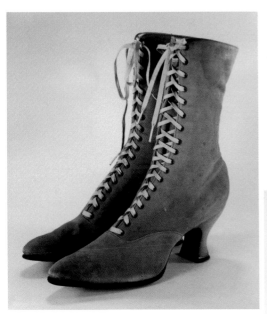

Left:
Pale gray suede high shoe or boot, front laced with 18 eyelets; lined with ivory cotton twill; silver stamped on kid inside top of right boot, "SOYSTER SHOE CO., Altoona, PA;" brown leather sole with 2-1/2-inch Louis XV heel, 1905-1910. *Courtesy of DUHCC.* $375-400.

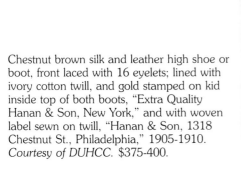

Chestnut brown silk and leather high shoe or boot, front laced with 16 eyelets; lined with ivory cotton twill, and gold stamped on kid inside top of both boots, "Extra Quality Hanan & Son, New York," and with woven label sewn on twill, "Hanan & Son, 1318 Chestnut St., Philadelphia," 1905-1910. *Courtesy of DUHCC.* $375-400.

Tan flannel and leather high shoe or boot; front laced with 18 eyelets; lined with ivory cotton twill, and stamped inside top of right boot, "Made In Boston, U.S.A., Dorothy Dodd;" and tan leather sole with 2-inch stacked heel with, "O'Sullivans Safety Heel" embossed on both heels, 1905-1910. *Courtesy of DUHCC.* $375-400.

Ivory canvas bathing shoe with ties; stamped on the canvas sole, "REG. U.S. PAT. OFF. OCEAN DIP BATHING SHOES, 6025," 1890-1910. $85-95.

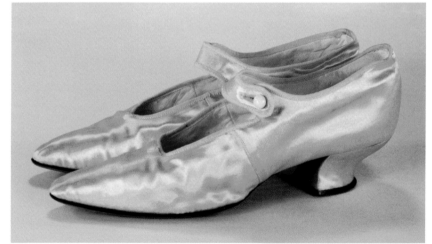

Brown leather high shoe or boot, front laced with 18 eyelets; lined with ivory cotton twill; brown leather sole with a 2-inch stacked heel, 1905-1910. *Courtesy of DUHCC.* $275-325.

Ivory silk satin low pointed toe shoe or slipper, with a single strap over the instep, fastened with a button; lightweight tan leather sole with a 1-inch baby Louis heel; lined with ivory kid, and silver stamped on right insole, "John Wanamaker, Phila., Paris, New York," 1900-1905. *Courtesy of DUHCC.* $95-125.

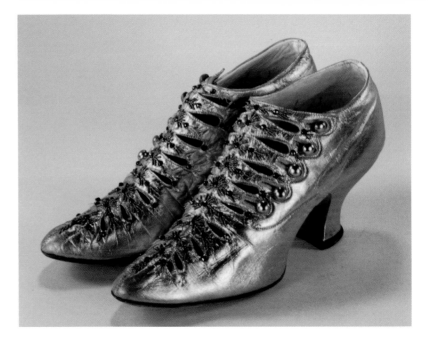

Iridescent brown low pointed toe shoe or slipper, with a decorative buckle on the vamp, set with pink crystal, and a tan leather sole with a 2-3/4-inch Louis XV heel; left insole gold stamped, "G. MOYKOPF, Burlington Arcade, LONDON W," 1905-1910. *Courtesy of DUHCC.* $275-300.

Gold kid low shoe or slipper, decorated with gold glass beads and cut onyx on vamp and five straps that cross the instep, and fasten with gold buttons.; lined with ivory kid; tan leather sole with 3-inch Louis XV heel, 1900-1905. *Purchased by the author from the Estate of Bertha K. Hershey.* $850-1000.

Black silk and black damask low shoe or slipper, with a single strap over the instep that fastens with a black glass button, lined with black kid, gold stamped on right insole, "N. Snellenburg & Co., PHILADELPHIA;" black leather sole with 2-1/2-inch Louis XV heel, 1905-1910. $275-325.

Left:
Photograph of the gold kid low
shoes, showing the
2-3/4-inch Louis XV heel.

Showing how the buttons fasten
the gold kid low shoes.

Gold kid low shoe or slipper, decorated
with amber and gold glass beads on
vamp, and four straps that cross the
instep, and fasten with gold buttons; lined
with ivory kid, with woven label,
"SOROSIS Trade Mark, Luxuries Made In
U.S.A.," 1905-1910. *Courtesy of
DUHCC*. $900-950.

Iridescent purple kid low shoe or slipper, decorated with iridescent copper beads on the vamp and four straps that cross the instep and fasten with purple buttons; lined with tan kid, and gold stamped on right insole, "N. Snellenburg & Co., Philadelphia;" tan leather sole with 2-3/4-inch Louis XV heel, 1900-1910. $425-450.

Burgundy suede and leather high shoe or boot, with decorative perforations and stitching on vamp and upper; front laced with 18 eyelets; lined with ivory cotton twill and burgundy silk faille, gold stamped, "SOROSIS, REG. U.S. PAT. OFF;" black leather sole with 2-3/4-inch Louis XV heel, 1900-1910. $650-700.

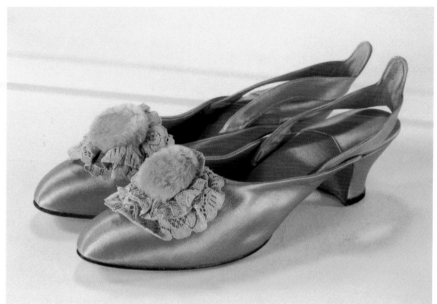

Pale peach silk satin slingback slipper, with fur and hand-made silk lace rosette on vamp; lined with peach silk satin; tan leather sole with 1-inch baby Louis heel, 1900-1905. It is rare to find a slingback style in this period. $325-350.

Ivory silk satin low shoe or slipper, decorated on vamp and around upper with clear glass beads; lined with pale gray kid, gold stamped on right insole, "Strawbridge & Clothier, Philadelphia;" tan leather sole with a 2-1/2-inch Louis XV heel, 1905-1910. $325-350.

1910s

Tan wool twill and black patent leather high shoe or boot, fastened on the side with 9 glass buttons; lined with ivory cotton twill, gold stamped on lining, "I. MILLER, W. 42nd Street, 1554 46 Way;" black leather sole with a 2-1/2 Louis XV heel, 1912-1915. *Courtesy of DUHCC.* $325-375.

Black leather and wool flannel high shoe or boot, fastened on the side with 11 glass buttons; lined with ivory cotton twill and leather; gold stamped inside top of right shoe, "Steigerwalt Boot Shop, Philadelphia, PA;" black leather sole with 2-inch heel, 1910-1915. *Courtesy of DUHCC.* $350-400.

Black silk satin low shoe or slipper, with a black leather sole and a 2-3/4 Louis XV heel; both insoles gold stamped, "J. & J. Slater, New York, 1910-1915. *Courtesy of DUHCC.* $95-110.

Black patent leather low shoe or pump, with a floral decoration of dull black glass beads mixed with silver steel beads; gold stamped on insole, "SOYSTER SHOE CO., ALTOONA, PA:" black leather sole with 2-1/2-inch flange heel, 1910-1915. *Courtesy of DUHCC.* $95-110.

Black patent leather low shoe or pump, decorated with a silver filigree buckle; tan leather sole with 2-3/4-inch flange heel; gold stamped on left insole, "Makers to the Royal Family, Hook Knowles & Co., 66 & 65 New Bond St., London," 1910-1915. *Courtesy of DUHCC.* $175-225.

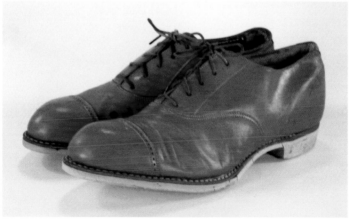

Black kid low shoe or slipper, with a single strap over the instep that fastens with a black glass button; elaborately decorated with diminutive dull black glass beads, on vamp and strap; 2-3/4-inch Louis XV heel, 1910-1915. $150-175.

Pale gray low shoe or pump, elaborately decorated on vamp with silver steel beads; lined with ivory kid, gold stamped, "Laird Schober and Co., Philada:" tan leather sole with a 2-1/2-inch Louis XV heel, 1900-1905. *Courtesy of DUHCC.* $325-375.

Tan leather oxford, with decorative stitching and perforations on vamp and across instep; lined with ivory cotton twill; white hard rubber sole, with 1-inch flat heel, 1910-1915. Possibly women's sports shoe, for bicycling, croquet, or golf. $95-125.

Left:
Tan suede and leather oxford, with decorative perforations on leather on vamp and across instep; lined with ivory cotton twill; brown leather sole with 2-inch stacked heel; stamped on both insoles, "Walk Over Trade Mark, REG. U.S. PAT. OFF., Custom Made," 1910-1915. Women's sports shoe. *Courtesy of DUHCC.* $150-175.

Bottom left:
Gray suede and brown leather oxford, with decorative perforations on leather on vamp and across instep; lined with ivory cotton twill; brown leather sole with 2-inch stacked heel; stamped on both insoles, "Walk Over Trade Mark, REG. U.S. PAT. OFF., Custom Made," 1910-1915. Women's sports shoe. *Courtesy of DUHCC.* $165-195.

Below:
Red kid T-strap low shoe or pump, with open-work and stitching on the shank, reminiscent of "spider webs;" lined with ivory kid, stamped on insole, "N. Snellenburg & Co.," tan leather sole with 2-3/4-inch Louis XV heel, 1910-1915. $325-375.

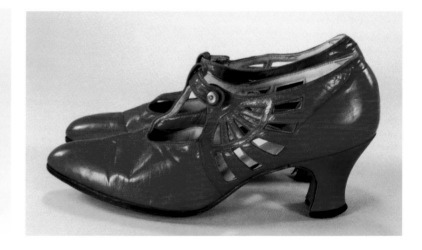

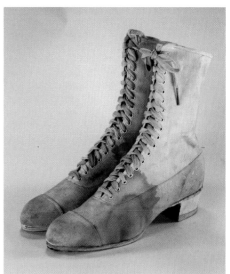

Brown leather high shoe or boot, with perforations and decorative stitiching on vamp; front laced with 15 eyelets; lined with ivory cotton twill; brown leather sole with 2-inch stacked heel, 1910-1915. $275-325.

White canvas high shoe or boot, front laced with eighteen eyelets; white hard rubber sole, with 1-inch heel, 1910-1915. *Women's sports shoe.* $275-325.

Left:
Gray suede high shoe or boot, fastened on the side with 14 buttons; lined with ivory cotton twill and ivory kid, gold stamped inside top, "Walk Over Custom Made;" tan leather sole with imprint of "Walk Over" and a 2-inch stacked heel, 1910-1915. $350-375.

Photograph showing the fronts of tan boots, with elaborate shoe buttons.

Tan leather high shoe or boot, with decorative perforations across the vamp; fastened on the side with 13 buttons; lined with ivory twill; brown leather sole with sturdy 1-inch stacked heel, 1910-1915. $200-225.

Brown suede low shoe or pump, with decorative perforations on upper, and tie closure; pointed toe, leather sole and 3-inch flange heel, with a metal heel lift, 1910-1915. $95-110.

1920s

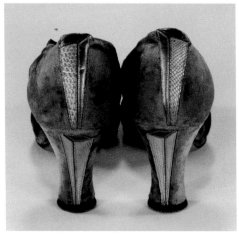

My mother loved to dance the Charleston. She had been very young in the 1920s, marrying my father in 1927. Years later she would be busy doing something in the house, and suddenly she would begin dancing the Charleston. As a little girl, I would join in. Her feet moved like liquid across the floor. It was a very energetic dance!

I remember my mother's dancing when I consider the fashion shoes of the 1920s. Women do not save their everyday shoes, or clothing for that matter. So, most of the examples of 1920s footwear that we have are fashion shoes. Although incredibly beautiful, even opulent, compared with other decades, the 1920s shoes were designed for stepping out, dancing the Charleston. They are beautiful, durable shoes.

Green velvet ankle strap pump, decorated on vamp with gold kid and silver lizard; right insole imprinted, "SAKS FIFTH AVENUE;" tan leather sole with 3-inch heel, also decorated with gold kid and silver lizard. *Courtesy of Karen Augusta.* $375-400.

The green velvet pumps, showing the open shank, ankle strap with green mother-of-pearl button, and vamp decorated with gold kid and silver lizard.

47

Brown silk satin pump, with a buckle on the vamp; tan leather sole with a 2-3/4-inch Louis XV heel. *Courtesy of DUHCC.* $95-125.

Right:
Black crepe dress with a pumpkin crepe drape, decorated in a floral pattern with black sequins, worn with a pumpkin horsehair hat, lined with ivory silk crepe, and decorated with same color silk flowers. The shoes are 1920s black silk pumps with silver filigree buckles. *Modeled by Tess Stewart.*

Black silk pump, with silver filigree buckle; gold stamped on right insole, "Winkelman;" tan leather sole with 2-1/2-inch French heel. $95-100.

Silver kid evening pump, hand-painted in a floral pattern, with a wide strap over the instep, decorated with a hand-painted buckle; gold stamped on right insole, "SAKS FIFTH AVENUE," and on left, "Fenton Footwear;" tan leather sole with 3-inch Louis XV heel. *Courtesy of DUHCC.* $275-300.

Gold and ivory brocade pump, with a single gold kid strap across the instep, attaching to a mother-of-pearl button, and gold kid decoration on the upper; gold stamped on both insoles, "Strawbridge & Clothier, Philadelphia;" tan leather sole with 3-1/2-inch gold kid heel. *Courtesy of DUHCC.* $325-375.

Brocade evening slipper or pump, in shades of lilac, blue, pink and gold, with a silver kid strap over the instep, fastened with a button; woven label, "HOOK KNOWLES & CO. LTD. 65-22 Bond ST WI, BY APPOINTMENT TO H. M. THE QUEEN;" tan leather sole with a 2-3/4-inch Louis XV heel, covered in silver kid. *Courtesy of DUHCC.* $275-325.

1930s

Many of the 1920s styles carried into the 1930s and, based on the evidence, there were plenty of evening shoes. Women had few pairs of shoes by contemporary standards, but relatively large numbers of evening shoes have survived. "T-strap" styles in gold or silver kidskin, or ivory satin, were most popular. It is curious that the United States of America was suffering in poverty as never before in history, and we have some incredible examples of women's fashion shoes to show for it.

Today, shoe designers have reinterpreted styles from the 1920s and 1930s, particularly for evening wear. Women who collect vintage 1930s gowns also love the "T-strap" evening pumps to wear with them. Condition is the most important factor to consider when buying vintage shoes to wear. Some collectors swoon over shoes by particular designers. For example, a pair of Salvatore Ferragamo shoes from the 1930s is a great find, and one could expect to pay a high price for such shoes. However, because most collectors buy shoes from the 1930s and 1940s to wear, designer name is perhaps secondary to size, condition, and style. Shoe designers may buy shoes in less than perfect condition, because it is their intention to redesign or reinterpret the shoes. The majority of women's fashion shoes made between 1930 and 1950 are beautifully crafted. Each shoe company employed talented designers, and great workmanship was a matter of pride.

Crocheted evening slipper, in shades of burgundy and black, with a 2-3/4-inch gold kid heel, gold kid trim, and narrow strap across the instep; right insole gold stamped, "Lord & Taylor," left insole gold stamped "Ferragamo." *Courtesy of Liz McGarrity.* $225-275.

Ivory silk slipper, embroidered with flowers and butterflies in shades of blue, lilac, rose, and green satin, with a 2-inch heel, and a thin brown leather sole; lined with cotton twill; stamped in black on lining of both shoes, "MADE IN CHINA, 625195." *Courtesy of Liz McGarrity.* $145-160.

Navy blue suede shoe, or fashion boot, with a high mesh vamp, decorated with suede braid and tiny steel rivets, with a 4-inch heel, and a black leather sole; both insoles gold stamped, "Phil.Tosk, Inc., Fine Quality Shoes, 3527 Broadway, New York City, 1311 Fulton St., Brooklyn, N.Y."*Courtesy of Liz McGarrity.* $225-285.

The navy blue suede shoe, or fashion boot. Notice the suede braid appliqué on the mesh, and the tiny steel rivets.

53

Top left:
Black leather pump, with a single strap across the instep, fastened with a button, and decorative perforations on the quarter; gold stamped on both insoles, "Craddock-Terry Co., Lynchburg, VA;" black leather sole with a 3-1/4-inch boulevard heel. *Courtesy of Mary Efron.* $95-105.

Above:
Black silk T-strap evening pump or slipper, with floral satin embroidery in shades of gold and amber on the vamp and heel; gold stamped on the left insole, "BONWIT TELLER, PHILADELPHIA;" tan leather sole with a 3-inch boulevard heel. *Courtesy of DUHCC.* $350-375.

Left:
Showing embroidery on the heels.

Burgundy silk opera pump, with a woven "Mary Jane" label on the right insole; tan leather sole with 3-1/2-inch French heel. $95-110.

Ivory silk pump, with decorative stitching on vamp; gold stamped on right insole, "mademoiselle T. M. REG. by Carlisle," and on the left, "The May Company, DENVER;" tan leather sole with 3-1/2-inch French heel. $95-110.

Burgundy silk opera pumps, with "Mary Jane" label.

Opposite page:
Red velvet evening coat, worn with a natural straw hat, decorated with red silk poppies. The shoes are 1930s burgundy velvet pumps.
Modeled by Tess Stewart.

Burgundy velvet evening pump; gold stamped on right insole, "Combination Last, Narrow Heel;" tan leather sole with 3-1/2-inch Continental heel. $95-115.

Black silk pump, with stitched silver kid "shield" on the vamp, decorated with rhinestones; gold stamped on both insoles, "SAKS FIFTH AVENUE, Fenton FOOTWEAR; tan leather sole with 3-3/4-inch silver kid French heel. $125-150.

Black silk pump, with a brass buckle on the vamp, and decorative openings on the upper; tan leather sole with 3-inch boulevard heel. $95-115.

Showing the silver kid French heel, decorated with a stitched "shield" and a rhinestone "diamond."

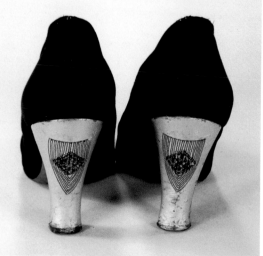

58

Brown leather pump, with decorative stitching and two small buttons on the vamp; gold stamped on right insole, "Naturalizer, The Shoe With The Beautiful Fit;" tan leather sole with 3-inch Cuban heel. $40-45.

Burgundy suede open-shank, T-strap pump, with decorative stitching on the vamp; tan leather sole with 3-1/2-inch boulevard heel. $85-95.

Brown suede open-toed, slingback pump, with small decorative holes on the vamp; gold stamped on both insoles, "Paradise Shoes;" tan leather sole with 3-3/4-inch French heel. $85-95.

Brown suede pump, with decorative stitching on the vamp and quarter, and a leather bow on the vamp; gold stamped on both insoles, "MILGRIM;" tan leather sole with 3-inch French heel. $85-95.

Rust suede pump, with decorative fringe on the vamp; gold stamped on right insole, "PALTER DE LISO, INC., NEW YORK CITY;" and on left, "BONWIT TELLER, FIFTH AVENUE;" tan leather sole with a 2-1/2-inch Cuban heel. *Courtesy of DUHCC.* $95-125.

Royal blue silk satin ankle-strap evening sandal or slipper, with decorative openings on the vamp; gold stamped on the right insole, "Betty Howard Fashions, Hutzler Brothers Co.;" tan leather sole with a 3-3/4-inch boulevard heel. $85-100.

Blue kid and tan, rose, and blue floral printed kid evening pump or slipper, with decorative openings on the vamp; gold stamped on insoles, "Frank Brothers Footwear, Fifth Avenue, New York;" tan leather sole with a 3-inch French heel. *Courtesy of DUHCC.* $325-375.

The floral printed leather sandal from the side, showing the French heel.

Left:
Silver kid T-strap evening pump or slipper, with decorative openings on the vamp and quarter; gold stamped on the right insole, "Nisley, Last 165;" tan leather sole with a 2-3/4-inch modified boulevard heel. $95-125.

Silver kid and ivory satin evening sandal or slipper, with an elaborately "twisted" ankle strap, and rhinestones on the buckle; gold stamped on velvet insoles, "SAKS FIFTH AVENUE, Fenton De Luxe;" tan leather sole with a 3-1/4-inch French heel. *Courtesy of DUHCC.* $375-425.

Showing the heel and ankle strap of the silver and gold kid evening sandal.

Tan lizard and black silk evening pump, with open-shank and open work on vamp, created by "layering" of straps; gold stamped on right insole, "Henri Bendel, New York," and on left, "Exclusively For Debusschere;" tan leather sole with 3-1/2-inch boulevard heel. *Courtesy of DUHCC.* $275-300.

Dark green alligator and suede pump, with decorative opening over the instep, and a tan leather sole with a 3-inch boulevard heel. $95-115.

Left:
White suede open-toed pump or wedgie, with a 3-inch black leather wedge-heel, and a black leather "string" bow on vamp; stamped on left insole, "Footwear Designed By Kalmon." $55-60.

63

Above:
Blue silk T-strap evening pump, with decorative openings on the vamp; gold stamped on right insole, "S. G. Nisley Lasted;" tan leather sole with a 3-inch modified Louis XV heel. *Courtesy of DUHCC.* $95-125.

Top right:
Gold kid open-toed, ankle-strap evening sandal or slipper, shown with pink velvet "toe pillows;" tan leather sole with a 3-inch boulevard heel. *Courtesy of DUHCC.* $95-105.

Right:
Open-toed, ankle-strap silver mesh sandal, with a woven label on right insole, "French Room Footwear, Sold Exclusively by Chandlers;" tan leather sole with a 3-1/2-inch boulevard heel. *Courtesy of DUHCC.* $95-125.

Blue silk T-strap evening pump or slipper, with decorative perforations on the vamp; gold stamped on right insole, "I. Miller Beautiful Shoes, Made in New York;" tan leather sole with a 3-inch modified Louis XV heel. *Courtesy of DUHCC.* $150-175.

Purple silk and satin evening pump or slipper, with elaborate contouring of fabric and appliqué on vamp and quarter; gold stamped on insoles, "Steigerwalt Boot Shop, Phila., PA;" tan leather sole with 3-inch modified Louis XV heel. *Courtesy of DUHCC.* $250-275.

Silver and gold kid, T-strap evening sandal or slipper, with decorative openings on vamp and quarter; gold stamped on insoles, "Steigerwalt Boot Shop, Chestnut St., Phila. PA;" tan leather sole with 3-inch modified Louis XV heel. *Courtesy of DUHCC.* $325-350.

Above:
Black and red silk faille ankle-strap evening pump or slipper, trimmed with gold kid, with zigzags on the vamp and quarter; gold stamped on right insole, "Made Exclusively For Geutings, Philadelphia;" tan leather sole with 2-1/2-inch baby Louis XV heel. *Courtesy of DUHCC.* $325-350.

Top left:
Iridescent purple kid pump, with a tan leather sole and a 2-1/2-inch Cuban heel. *Courtesy of DUHCC.* $65-75.

Left:
Iridescent purple kid evening pump or slipper, with decorative perforations on vamp and quarter; gold stamped on right insole, "Made Expressly For I. Miller," and on left, "Ingenue Model;" tan leather sole with a 3-inch boulevard heel. *Courtesy of DUHCC.* $95-105.

Black silk pump, with "diamond" openings on vamp, trimmed with gold kid, and tied over the instep with wide, black laces; gold stamped on right insole, "Laird Schober & Co., Philada.," and on left, "NAPIER'S;" tan leather sole with a 3-inch boulevard heel. *Courtesy of DUHCC.* $85-95.

Suede evening pump or slipper, in shades of green, pink, mauve, gray, and yellow; decorative crossing colored straps for dramatic effect, including a green ankle strap through a pale pink suede quarter; gold stamped on right insole, "Murray's Smart Shoes, 916 Chestnut Street, Phila.," and on left, "Combination Last, Narrow Heel;" tan leather sole with a 3-1/2-inch modified boulevard heel. *Courtesy of DUHCC.* $175-225.

Ivory velvet T-strap evening pump or slipper, with decorative perforations on the vamp and the quarter; gold stamped on right insole, "I. MILLER Beautiful Shoes, 115 Lasts Made in New York," and on left, "I. Miller Sons, Inc. REG. U.S. PAT. OFF.;" tan leather sole with a 3-inch Louis XV heel. *Courtesy of DUHCC.* $275-325.

Right:
Brown suede open-toed pump, with laces, and decorative stitching and perforations on the vamp and across instep; tan leather sole with 3-3/4-inch Cuban heel. $55-60.

Brown suede pump, with decorative stitching and small buttons on the vamp; gold stamped on right insole, "SHOES OF THE HOUR by Nisley;" brown leather sole with a 3-1/2-inch boulevard heel. $85-95.

Pale green brocade slingback, wedge-soled slipper, with silver kid trim, and a tan leather sole, imprinted, "Made in China." *Courtesy of the Estate of Elizabeth P. Fischer.* $125-175.

Showing the back of the Ferragamo shoe.

Black silk faille wedge-soled, ankle-strap evening sandal, with an open-shank; trimmed on the vamp and wedge heel with silver kid; gold stamped on the right insole, "FERRAGAMO CREATIONS, Florence, Italy," and on the left, "SAKS FIFTH AVENUE. *The vamp is designed in gores, and the quarter extends high up on the ankle, and accommodates the silver kid ankle strap, also known as bracelet tie. Courtesy of DUHCC.* $275-350.

Showing the 3-1/4-inch wedge heel and quarter.

Brown leather and ivory pigskin wedgie, with front laces; gold stamped on insoles, "MADE BY Premier, NEW YORK-PARIS;" tan leather sole with 3-1/4 wedge heel. $95-115.

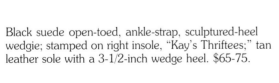

Black suede open-toed, ankle-strap, sculptured-heel wedgie; stamped on right insole, "Kay's Thriftees;" tan leather sole with a 3-1/2-inch wedge heel. $65-75.

Light tan open-shank, T-strap pump; gold stamped on both insoles, "Franklin Simon & Co., FIFTH AVE. NEW YORK, Customized;" tan leather sole with 3-inch French heel. $85-95.

Black silk T-strap evening sandal or slipper; gold stamped on right insole, "Custom Shoes Made By Hand For The Blum Store, Philadelphia," and on left, "PALTER DE LISO., INC., NEW YORK CITY;" tan leather sole with a 3-1/4 boulevard heel. *Courtesy of DUHCC.* $95-115.

Lilac silk satin T-strap evening sandal or slipper, with a tan leather sole and a 2-1/2-inch modified boulevard heel. *Courtesy of DUHCC.* $95-125.

Open-toed, woven fabric sandal in shades of red, yellow, black, and orange; ankle-strap ties with multi-colored string; lined with ivory kid; tan leather sole with 3-inch Cuban heel, from South America or Costa Rica. *Courtesy of Mary Efron.* $95-115.

Navy blue leather open-toed, open-shank, ankle-strap sandal, with a tan leather sole and 3-1/4-inch boulevard heel. $75-85.

Gold mesh open-toed mule, with green, blue, and red stripes, and a gold leather strap on the vamp; stamped on insoles, "Strawbridge & Clothier, Philadelphia;" tan leather sole with a 3-inch Cuban heel. $65-75.

Left:
Brown alligator pump, with decorative "fringe" across the vamp; gold stamped on right insole, "dewees, PHILADELPHIA," and on left, "Ronney, Styled For Dewees;" tan leather sole with 3-1/2-inch Cuban heel. $85-95.

Tan and brown open-toed snakeskin pump; gold stamped on left insole, "GENUINE Python;" tan leather sole with 3-1/2-inch boulevard heel. $95-115.

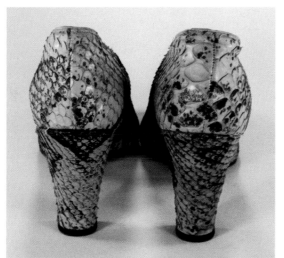

Showing the heels of the python pumps.

Right:
Open-toed, slingback ivory polka-dot linen pump, with a bow on the vamp; gold stamped on right insole, "Paramount FOOTWEAR DESIGNED BY Kalmon," and on left, "Farr's ALLENTOWN, EASTON, BETHLEHEM, READING;" tan leather sole with a 4-inch boulevard heel. $95-110.

Tan and brown open-toed snakeskin (python) pump; with a tan leather sole and a 3-1/2-inch boulevard heel. $95-115.

Right:
Navy blue grosgrain ribbon mesh pump; gold stamped on pink kid insoles, "SAKS FIFTH AVENUE Fenton FOOTWEAR;" black leather sole with a 3-1/2-inch French heel, covered with navy blue faille. $85-95.

Black faille wedge-soled, open-toed slipper, with elastic straps across the open-shank, and a striped satin low platform and wedge-heel; gold stamped on the right insole, "Blum;" tan vinyl sole. $40-45.

Blue linen open-toed, open-shank pump, with an "eyelet" design on the vamp, and a tan leather sole with a 3-inch French heel. $65-75.

Black suede open-toed pump, with decorative perforations and grosgrain ribbons and bows on the vamp; labeled on the right insole, "BEAUTIFUL NANETTE CEM-PRO SHOES;" tan leather sole with a 2-1/2-inch boulevard heel. $40-45.

Navy blue leather open-toe pump, with a navy blue and white leather decorative "knot" on the vamp; gold stamped on right insole, "Tweedies Alluring Footwear," and on left, "Quality Boot Shop, Philipsburg, PA;" tan leather sole with a 3-inch boulevard heel. $45-48.

Purple iridescent leather bracelet tie pump, with an additional strap over the instep; both straps are fastened with buttons; gold stamped on right insole, " Customcraft Originals, Styled by SCHWARTZ-BEN-JAMIN," and on left, "John Wanamaker;" black leather sole with 4-inch French heel. $65-70.

Black and iridescent gray leather ankle-strap, open-toe sandal; gold stamped on right insole, "Tweedies Alluring Footwear," and on left, "Gittleman's in Williamsport;" black leather sole with a 4-inch Spanish heel. $50-55.

Above left::
Black leather pump, with black fabric upper, and decorative leather bows on the vamp; black leather sole with a 3-1/2-inch Cuban heel. $45-50.

Above:
Burgundy silk satin open-toed, open-shank, ankle-strap evening sandal; imprinted on insole, "Flevan Bros., Altoona, Harrisburg;" tan leather sole with a 3-inch French heel. $95-115.

Left:
Black suede and leather pump, with laces over the instep, and tan lizard appliqué; gold stamped on right insole, "BAKER'S, BROCKTON, MASS.;" black leather sole with a 2-1/2-inch modified boulevard heel. $95-115.

Vintage Footwear

1940s

As a collector, I love the diversity of the 1940s fashion shoes. I particularly love the "platform sandals," which are beautifully crafted. Each subsequent time that platform shoes have come into fashion—in the late 1960s and early 1970s, and again in the mid-1990s, they have lost something in translation. The 1940s platforms always have leather soles and leather insoles, and the ankle straps have a precision that has not been duplicated in the later versions.

The war years affected fashion. My mother could not get nylon or silk stockings, but she managed to look very fashionable in ankle socks, which she often wore with platform sandals, or with "wedge-soled" sandals made of canvas. I am certain that she wore out a few pairs of shoes during the war, but like most women of that time, she wore whatever she had in the closet. Women did not throw out their shoes, or donate them to the Salvation Army, the way they do today. Many women were wearing low-heeled oxfords or plain, rounded-toe pumps to go with their man-tailored, wool gabardine suits. It was a very practical time.

The market is strong for the 1940s platform sandals, particularly in reptile or suede. Many women, who enjoy wearing the beautifully tailored gabardine suits of the period, collect 1940s pumps to wear with their suits.

Opposite page:
Tan and brown wool challis suit, with a pleated skirt. Worn with a tan felt hat, decorated with a black feather and veil. The shoes are brown alligator open-toed, slingback pumps, with laces. *Modeled by Bridget Foy.*

Brown alligator open-toed, slingback pump, with laces over instep; silver stamped on both insoles, "GENUINE SHENANIGAN ALLIGATOR;" tan leather sole with 1-1/2-inch heel, similar to Cuban heel, but with a curved breast. $95-115.

Ivory silk slip, trimmed with handmade silk lace. The boudoir slippers are 1940s burgundy satin open-toe mules, with burgundy satin rosettes on the vamp. *Modeled by Adria Hadley.*

Burgundy satin open-toe
mule, with rosettes on the
vamp, and a 3-inch fabric
covered heel; silver
stamped on satin insole,
"Daniel Green, Made in U.
S. A." $85-95. *Courtesy of
Mary Efron.*

Dark green suede open-toed pump, with an open-shank look on one side only, and a single strap across the instep; decorative perforations on vamp and strap; silver stamped on right insole, "Cricketts;" tan leather sole with 2-inch common sense heel, covered in green leather. $95-115.

Top right:
Tan lizard open-toed, ankle-strap sandal, with decorative "layering" on the vamp; gold stamped on right insole, "Tweedies Alluring Footwear, Iguana Lizard," and on left, "QUALITY BOOT SHOP, PHILIPSBURG, PA;" black leather sole with 3-1/4-inch boulevard heel. $95-115.

Right:
Tan Iguana lizard handbag which matches the sandals. $85-90.

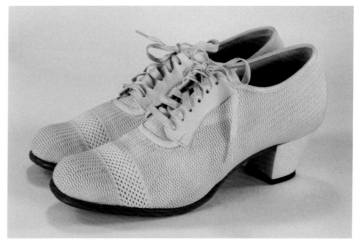

Left:
Black suede open-toed, slingback pump, with a double-strap over the instep; labeled on right insole, "RED CROSS SHOE, THE UNITED STATES SHOE CORP; REG. U.S. PAT. OFF.;" tan leather sole with a 3-1/4-inch Cuban heel. $45-50.

Bright yellow mesh and leather Mamma shoe, or lace-up oxford, with tan leather sole and a 2-inch common sense heel. $45-48.

Left:
Navy blue open-toed, slingback pump, with a strap over the instep, and decorative perforations on the vamp; gold stamped on insoles, "Selby ARCH PRESERVES;" black leather sole with a 3-inch boulevard heel. $40-45.

Navy blue leather Mamma shoe, or lace-up oxford, with decorative perforations on the vamp and across the instep, a black leather sole, and a 2-inch common sense heel; silver stamped on both insoles, "Selby Arch Preservers." $40-45

Purple silk faille open-toed pump, with a purple silk rosette on the vamp; black leather sole with a 3-inch modified boulevard heel. *Courtesy of DUHCC.* $85-95.

Left:
Navy blue fabric overshoe, with black fur trim, and side-zipper; labeled "Glove Originals" on the molded rubber sole. $55-60.

Photograph of two pairs of Mamma shoes, or lace-up oxfords, including tan mesh with brown leather, gold stamped on the right insole, "Royal Foot Defenders," and tan and brown leather. Both pairs have tan leather soles, with 2-inch common sense heels. $45-48, per pair.

Photograph of two pairs of Mamma shoes, or lace-up oxfords, including white mesh with leather, stamped on right insole, "Styled by Emma Jettick," and black leather, with decorative stitching on the vamp and perforations over the instep. Both pairs have leather soles with 2-inch common sense heels. $45-48, per pair.

Right:
Black velvet overshoe, with black fur trim, front laces, and a plaid flannel lining; stamped on the molded rubber sole, "Gaytees." $65-70.

Black velvet overshoe, with black fur trim, and a side-zipper; lined with tan flannel, and labeled "B. F. Goodrich" on the molded rubber sole. $65-70.

Tan mesh and brown leather open-toed, slingback pump; silver stamped on both insoles, "Miracle-Tread, Cushioned;" tan leather sole with a 3-inch boulevard heel. $45-48.

Navy blue suede ankle-strap pump, with a wide strap and large buckle; gold stamped on right insole, "Sophisticates by HALBRO;" tan leather sole with a 2-3/4-inch Cuban heel. *Courtesy of DUHCC.* $85-95.

Showing the unusual ankle strap.

White suede open-toed, slingback sandal, with decorative perforations on the vamp; gold stamped on insoles, "Delman De Luxe, The best shoes you can buy are the best buy, New York, Chicago, London, Paris;" tan leather sole with 2-1/2-inch Cuban heel. *Courtesy of DUHCC.* $95-105.

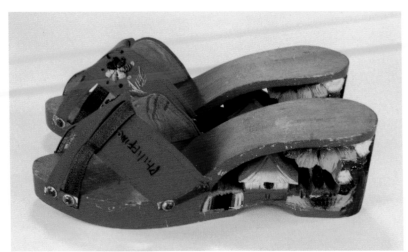

Wedge-soled, slip-on wood sandal, carved and painted with an island scene, including trees and houses; "Philippines" embroidered on the red fabric vamp. $125-150.

Showing a pair of wedge-soled, slip-on wood sandals for a child, carved and painted with an island scene; shown in front of an adult size sandal. $175-200.

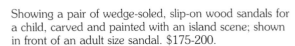

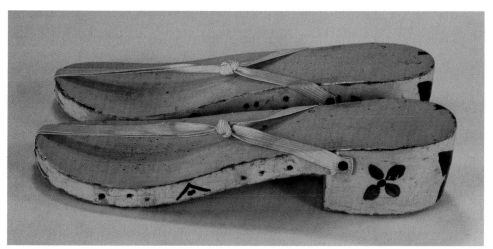

Yellow painted wood sandal, decorated with flowers and butterflies; elastic thong holds foot in place. $85-95.

The back of the yellow painted wood sandals, showing a blue and red painted butterfly.

Woven rope sandals for a young child, 6-1/2-inches long. $30-35.

Wedge-soled slip-on wood sandal, carved and colorfully painted with an island scene; the vamp is woven, and "Philippines 1945" is painted on the insole. These sandals are intricately carved and painted, never worn, and dated. $225-250.

The wood sandals, showing the date.

Wedge-soled slip-on wood sandal, with a green velvet vamp, beaded in a floral design, and with the word "Philippines" embroidered in white beads; carved through the wedge and colorfully painted, showing an island scene. $125-175.

Wedge-soled, ankle-strap wood sandal, carved all the way through the wedge, showing an island scene with trees and houses; black velvet vamp with floral embroidery; additionally painted in a floral pattern on the insole, and signed "Philippines." *Courtesy of Donna Sigler.* $175-200.

The wood sandal, showing the carving through the wedge, and the colorful embroidery on the black velvet vamp.

Avacado green leather open-toed, slingback platform pump; labeled on right insole, "RED CROSS SHOES, THE UNITED STATES SHOE CORP, REG. U.S. PAT. OFF.:" tan leather sole with 4-inch boulevard heel. $85-95.

Tan alligator open-toed, ankle-strap platform sandal, with decorative perforations on the vamp; gold stamped on the right insole, "MADE EXPRESSLY FOR Gimbel Brothers;" black leather sole with a 4-1/2-inch boulevard heel. $125-140.

Left:
Showing the heels and ankle-straps of the alligator platform sandals.

Navy blue suede ankle strap platform sandal, with decorative perforations lined with mesh on the vamp; gold stamped on the right insole, "House of Pierre HAND CRAFTED;" black leather sole with a 3-1/2-inch boulevard heel. $85-90.

Left:
Burgundy snakeskin, open-toed, ankle-strap platform sandal; gold stamped on right insole, "John Wanamaker," and on left, "Sky Lasts;" black leather sole with 3-3/4-inch French heel. $110-125.

Green suede open-toed, slingback platform pump, with decorative perforations and green kid "leaves" on the vamp; gold stamped on right insole, "Jacqueline designed by Wohl;" tan leather sole with 3-1/2-inch boulevard heel. $110-125.

Charcoal gray tweed suit, with a fitted jacket and a straight skirt. The shoes are 1940s tan alligator open-toed, slingback platform pumps. *Modeled by Emily Fischer. The 1931 Ford courtesy of Douglas and Lois Fischer*

Tan alligator open-toed, slingback platform pump, with decorative perforations on the vamp: gold stamped on right insole, "MADE EXPRESSLY FOR Gimbel Brothers," and on left, "Genuine Alligator;" black leather sole with 3-1/4-inch Cuban heel. $125-150.

Moss green suede open-toed, slingback platform pump, with decorative perforations on the vamp; gold stamped on left insole, "Urbanites by James Keans, New York City;" black leather sole with a 3-inch modified boulevard heel. *Courtesy of DUHCC*. $95-110.

Gold kid and black velvet open-toed, slingback platform evening sandal; with open "lattice" effect in gold kid and black velvet on the vamp; gold stamped on the right insole; "PALTER DE LISO, INC., NEW YORK CITY;" and on left "THE BLUM STORE, PHILADEL-PHIA;" black leather sole with 4-inch boulevard heel. $150-175.

Left:
Brown velvet and brown satin open-toed, ankle-strap platform evening sandal, decorated with brown satin on the vamp; imprinted on insoles, "SAKS FIFTH AVENUE;" black leather sole with 4-inch Continental heel. $110-125.

White suede and green kid open-toed, slingback platform pump, with a green "leaf" decoration on the vamp; gold stamped on right insole, "Valley Shoes," and on left, "BONWIT TELLER, PHILADELPHIA;" tan leather sole with 4-inch boulevard heel. *Courtesy of DUHCC.* $95-110.

Black suede open-toed, sling back pump, with red leather platform and heel, and a colorful leather "swirl" on vamp; gold stamped on right insole, "W. H. Steigerwalt, PHILADELPHIA, PA;" and on left, "PALTER DE LISO, INC., NEW YORK CITY;" tan leather sole with 4-inch modified boulevard heel. *Courtesy of DUHCC.* $125-175.

Red leather open-toed, slingback platform pump; gold stamped on right insole, "Marquise Originals;" tan leather sole with a 4-1/2-inch boulevard heel. *Courtesy of DUHCC.* $95-115.

Rust suede open-toed, slingback pump, with a brown kid flower on the vamp; gold stamped on right insole, "Frank Brothers Footwear, Inc., New York, Chicago;" and on left, "Sophistocrat;" tan leather sole with 4-inch boulevard heel. *Courtesy of DUHCC.* $95-110.

Opposite page:
Green wool gabardine suit, with dark green Bakelite buttons, worn with a wide-brimmed gray felt hat, and a multi-colored pouch-style crocheted pocketbook. The shoes are 1940s gray suede open-toed, ankle-strap platform sandals. *Modeled by Adria Hadley.*

Gray suede open-toed, ankle-strap platform sandal, with decorative cut out "diamonds" on the vamp; stamped on both insoles, "Barbara Gay Shoes;" tan leather sole with 4-inch boulevard heel. $115-125.

Tan suede and ivory mesh open-toed, ankle-strap platform sandal, with decorative suede "grapes" on the vamp; gold stamped on right insole, "Avonettes," and on left, "SAKS FIFTH AVENUE DEBU-TANTE FASHIONS;" tan leather sole with 4-inch French heel. $125-135.

Opposite page:
Pale blue silk velvet gown, worn with over-the-elbow ivory kid gloves, and a small ivory beaded clutch-style pocketbook. The shoes are 1940s white suede open-toed, double ankle-strap platform sandals. *Modeled by Adria Hadley.*

White suede open-toed, double ankle-strap platform sandal, with decorative openings and stitching on the vamp, and a tan leather sole with a 1-inch platform, and a 4-inch boulevard heel. $125-135.

Black suede open-toed, ankle-strap platform sandal, with decorative beading around "diamond" openings on vamp; gold stamped on right insole, "PALTER DE LISO, INC. NEW YORK CITY," and on left "BONWIT TELLER, FIFTH AVE.;" black leather sole with 3-1/2-inch boulevard heel. $110-125.

Black suede open-toed, ankle-strap platform sandal, decorated on vamp, heel, and platform with satin floral embroidery and iridescent gray-green glass beads; gold stamped on right insole, "Originals by De-Silva, Hand Made, New York," and on left, "METRO SHOE CO., INC., FINE FOOTWEAR;" black leather sole with 4-inch French heel. $300-350.

Open-toed, ankle-strap ivory silk satin platform sandal, elaborately decorated with rhinestones; decorative openings on the vamp; gold stamped on insoles, "Sommers of jay thorpe;" tan leather sole with 2-inch platform and 5-1/2-inch boulevard heel. *Courtesy of DUHCC.* $350-425.

Showing heels and ankle-straps of the ivory satin sandals.

Burgundy snakeskin and mesh open-toed, ankle-strap platform sandal, with floral snakeskin decoration on vamp; gold stamped on insole, "CUSTOM MADE," black leather sole with 1-inch platform and 4-inch French heel. $275-300.

Opposite page:
Tan crepe late day dress, with drape and flounce, and cooper beading on the bodice. Worn with a wide-brimmed black silk velvet hat, with feathers. The shoes are 1940s black suede open-toed, ankle-strap platform sandals. *Modeled by Emily Fischer.*

Black suede open-toed, ankle-strap platform sandal, with metallic gold "almond" shapes decorating the high platform and heel; gold stamped on right insole, "design by Evins;" black leather sole with 5-inch square heel. $175-225.

Black suede open-toed, ankle-strap platform pump; gold stamped on right insole, "Air Step PATS. NO. 9682907, Magic Sole," and on left, "French Bootery, 1409 11th Avenue, Altoona, Pa.;" black leather sole with 4-inch boulevard heel. *Courtesy of Mary Efron.* $150-175.

Opposite page:
Purple and black woven silk gown, with smocking and silk velvet bows on the shoulders. Worn with short ivory crocheted gloves, with ivory kid palms. The shoes are 1940s black suede open-toed, ankle-strap platform sandals. *Modeled by Marcie Behanna.*

Black suede open-toed, ankle-strap platform sandal, with decorative perforations on the vamp; black leather sole with a 4-1/2-inch modified French heel. $115-125.

Brown suede open-toed, slingback pumps, with a copper kid "flower" on the vamp; gold stamped on insoles, "ingenue, Made For I. Miller;" tan leather sole with a 3-3/4-inch modified boulevard heel. *Courtesy of DUHCC*. $175-200.

Brown suede open-toed, slingback platform pump, with decorative perforations and beading on vamp; gold stamped on both insoles, "Another Cynthia Original, DUCHESS LAST;" tan leather sole with 1/2-inch platform and 4-inch boulevard heel. $150-175

Above:
Maroon iridescent kid open-toed, ankle-strap platform sandal, with decorative "knots" on the vamp; black leather sole with 4-inch modified French heel. $115-125.

Top right:
Green leather open-toed, ankle-strap platform pump, with decorative perforations and tiny buttons on the vamp; gold stamped on right insole, "Laird Schober Co., TRADE MARK," and on left, "John Wanamaker;" tan leather sole with 3-1/3 boulevard heel. $95-110.

Right:
Black suede open-toe pump, with perforations, a bow, and grosgrain ribbon decorations on the vamp; gold stamped on insoles, "Matrix Your Footprint in Leather;" black leather sole with 2-1/2-inch common sense heel. $40-45.

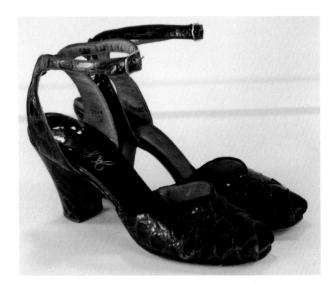

Brown alligator open-toed, ankle-strap sandal; gold stamped on right insole, "John Wanamaker, New York." *Courtesy of DUHCC.* $95-125.

Brown alligator pump, with a rounded toe and high-cut vamp; gold stamped on insoles, "ingenue, MADE FOR I. MILLER;" tan leather sole with 3-1/2-inch boulevard heel. *This style became popular in the late 1940s and continued into the early 1950s.* $95-125

Left:
Burgundy leather sling-back, open-shank pump, with four black buttons and decorative "scallops" on the vamp; gold stamped on right insole, "mademoiselle T.M. REG. Shoes," and on left, "Brozman's, Williamsport, PA;" black leather sole with a 3-1/2-inch modified boulevard heel. $85-95.

Open-toed, slingback sandal, in shades of rose, pale blue, and hot pink; gold stamped on right insole, "Dorian Originals," and on left, "Exclusive With Lit Brothers;" tan leather sole with a 4-inch modified boulevard heel. *Courtesy of DUHCC.* $125-150.

Side view, showing boulevard heel and laces.

Gold kid open-toed, slingback sandal, with straps across the vamp, and a tan leather sole with a 3-1/2-inch modified boulevard heel. *Courtesy of DUHCC.* $95-110.

Opposite page:
Striped wool gabardine suit, in shades of
mauve, tan, and brown. Worn with a
brown felt fedora-style hat, and a brown
clutch-style crocheted pocketbook. The
shoes are 1940s brown suede open-toed
pumps, with a brown suede bow on the
vamp. *Modeled by Francesca Stewart.*

Brown suede open-toed pump, with a
brown suede bow on the vamp; gold
stamped on right insole, "Sorority Group,
Hand Crafted;" tan leather sole with 4-
inch boulevard heel. $85-95.

Tan and brown leather open-toed, slingback wedgie, with small white crosses decorating the upper; stamped on right insole, "floaters REG. by Turian," and the left, "Charles Kushine;" tan leather sole with 2-3/4-inch wedge heel. *Courtesy of DUHCC.* $65-70.

Side view of wedge sole.

Showing "cross" design on wedge-heel.

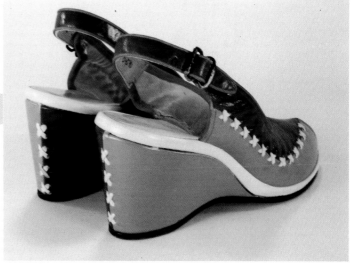

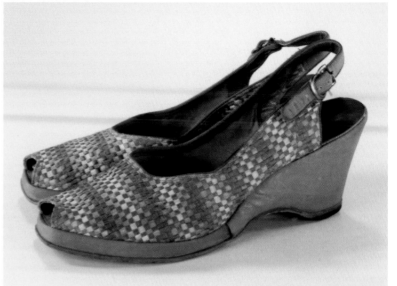

Brown lizard open-toed, ankle-strap pump; gold stamped on insoles, "Val Del CUSTOM FOOTWEAR;" tan leather sole with a 4-inch modified boulevard heel. *Courtesy of DUHCC.* $85-95.

Above right:
Gray and white woven linen open-toed, slingback wedgie; labeled on the right insole, "TOWN & COUNTRY SHOES," and stamped on the tan leather sole, "T & C'S RISING STAR;" 3-inch wedge-heel. $40-45.

Right:
Brown suede and tan leather open-toed, ankle-strap wedgie, with "saw tooth" decorations and cut-outs on the vamp; tan leather sole with a 3-inch wedge-heel. $45-48.

Black satin open-toed slipper, with a black leather sole and a 1-inch flat heel. $30-35.

Brown suede and mesh pump; gold stamped on right insole, "HAND CRAFTED House of Pierre," tan leather sole with a 3-1/2-inch modified French heel. $45-50.

Navy blue suede and mesh open-toed pump; gold stamped on right insole, "HAND CRAFTED House of Pierre;" black leather sole with a 3-1/2-inch modified French heel. $45-50.

Tan alligator open-toed, slingback pump; stamped on left insole, "Whippersnapper;" tan leather sole with 3-1/4-inch Cuban heel. Store name on right insole is illegible. $85-95.

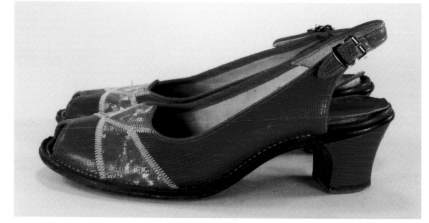

Tan and brown lizard open-toed, slingback pump, with a tan leather sole and a 2-inch Cuban heel. $48-50.

Brown alligator pump, with a rounded toe and stitching on the vamp; gold stamped on insoles, "Geuting's EMPIRE FASHIONS, PHILADELPHIA;" black leather sole with 4-inch modified French heel. $85-95.

Tan alligator pump, with a rounded toe and stitching on the vamp; gold stamped on the right insole, "Foot Delight SHOES," and on the left, "EXCLUSIVE WITH Lit Brothers, PHILADELPHIA;" tan leather sole with 3-inch modified French heel. $85-95.

Green leather pump, with decorative perforations around the upper; silver stamped on right insole, "HOFHEIMER'S Gay Craft SHOES;" black leather sole with 3-inch Cuban heel. $40-45.

Opposite page:
Gray and brown plaid wool suit, with a pleated skirt. Worn with a black wool pocketbook. The shoes are 1940s black suede open-toe pumps. *Modeled by Emily Fischer. 1931 Ford courtesy of Douglas and Lois Fischer.*

Black suede open-toed pump, with decorative "swirl" stitching and a button on the vamp; labeled on the right insole, "Natural Bridge Shoes;" black leather sole with a 2-1/2-inch Cuban heel. $45-50.

1950s

Pink and gray snakeskin pump, with "wrap" decoration and small button on the vamp; insoles gold stamped, "Pacelle SAKS FIFTH AVENUE;" tan leather sole with a 4-inch French heel. $48-55.

If there is one decade that yields large numbers of shoes for collectors, it is the 1950s. I can remember going into a shoe store with my mother, and watching her try on and purchase four or five pairs of suede high-heeled pumps, identical in all respects, except color! Women matched accessories as never before—pocketbooks and shoes in the same color and material. Hats and gloves further complimented the ensemble. It was a fashion decade like no other!

Women's fashion shoes of the early 1950s have rounded toes and relatively thick, high-heels. Mid-1950s shoes have slightly tapered toes, but not pointed, and thinner high-heels. By the end of the decade shoes have pointed toes, and either spike heels (high heel, narrow at the bottom) or stiletto heels (high set-back heel which ends in a tiny rounded base, usually fitted with a metal tip). Sling-back sandals of all descriptions were popular during the 1950s, including plastic sling-back sandals with Lucite (trademark of E. I. Du Pont de Nemours and Company for transparent acrylic plastic material) heels. This was also the decade of the slide sandal (toeless, open-back sandal with a heel in various heights) with the "Spring-O-Lator" insole (elastic piece attached to the insole to keep the shoe on the foot).

The market for the 1950s shoes is strong today among women who enjoy wearing the period's clothing for special occasions. Costume designers and stylists often find themselves looking for a particular pair of shoes to compliment a "look" for stage, screen, or print advertising.

Blue and ivory floral brocade pump; gold stamped on insoles, "andrew geller, exquisite footwear;" tan leather sole with a 3-1/2-inch French heel. $95-110.

Green snakeskin pump, with a decorative "swirl" on the vamp; gold stamped on right insole, "Enzel of Paris," and on the left, "Genuine Reptile, Our Famous 30 Last;" black leather sole with 4-inch French heel. $75-85.

Tan alligator pump, with modified open-shank look, and decorative stitching on the vamp; printing on insole is illegible; brown leather sole with 4-inch French heel. $65-85.

Purple iridescent leather pump, with low-cut vamp; gold stamped on insoles, "Delman De Luxe;" tan leather sole with a 3-1/2-inch boulevard heel. *Courtesy of DUHCC.* $85-95.

Red suede and black patent leather pump, with decorative perforations on the patent leather that "swirls" across the vamp; gold stamped on insoles, "Miss Pedestrienne by Gray Bros.;" black leather sole with 2-1/2-inch French heel. *Shown with a matching pocketbook.* $95-110.

Black suede pump, with open work and stitching on the vamp; labeled in right insole, "Red Cross Shoe, The United States Shoe Corr Reg. U.S. Pat. Off;" tan leather sole with 3-inch Cuban heel. $35-40.

Above left:
Gray suede pump, with white and gray leather braid around the upper; gold stamped on right insole, "Grayflex Footwear, REG. U.S. PAT. OFF.;" tan leather sole with a 2-3/4-inch stacked heel. *Courtesy of DUHCC.*

Above:
White suede and black patent leather pump, with button decoration on the vamp; gold stamped on right insole, "Custom Shoemaking by Anthony Mascioli, New York," and on left, "Tailored Woman, Fifth Avenue;" tan leather sole with a 3-1/2-inch French heel. *Courtesy of DUHCC.* $85-95.

Black suede open-toed, slingback platform pump, with interlocking straps making up the vamp; gold stamped on insoles, "EXQUISITE HERMAN'S FOOTWEAR;" black leather sole with a 4-inch boulevard heel. *Courtesy of DUHCC.* $55-65.

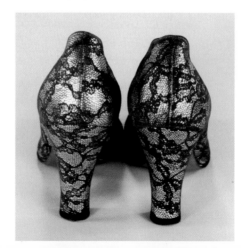

Blue and silver lace printed leather pump; gold stamped on the right insole, "VOGUE SHOE SHOP LTD., MOUNT ROYAL HOTEL, MONTREAL;" tan leather sole, stamped "Del Grande Hand Made," with a 4-inch French heel. *Courtesy of Matthew Smith.* $95-115.

Showing the heels of the blue and silver lace pumps.

Pale pink "dyed to match" satin pump, with 3-1/2-inch spike heel, shown with a rose and silver brocade pump; silver stamped, "Sophisticates by Halbro, Made in U.S.A., with a 2-inch Cuban heel. These styles were worn to proms and dances during the period.

The original "Pedwin" box for the 1950s blue suede oxfords.

Blue suede oxford, labeled on the right insole, "Pedwin SHOES FOR MEN;" tan leather sole with a flat heel. $75-85.

The original record, "Blue Suede Shoes," written and performed by Carl Perkins, for "Sun" records in Memphis, Tennessee. *Courtesy of Bruce Smith.*

Clear plastic slide with rhinestone decorations on vamp, a "Spring-O-Lator" insole, and a 4-inch Lucite spike heel. *Courtesy of DUHCC.* $50-55.

Two pairs of clear plastic slides, showing the Lucite heels. *Courtesy of DUHCC.*

This page:
Ivory net strapless gown,
decorated with hand
applied iridescent sequins
and clear rhinestones.
Worn with over-the-elbow
ivory kid gloves. Shoes are
clear plastic 1950s
slingback sandals, with
Lucite heels. *Modeled by
Marcie Behanna.*

Clear plastic open-toed, slingback sandal, with rhinestone decorations on the vamp; gold stamped on right insole, "The American Girl, T. M. REG. U. S. PAT. OFF., MADE IN U.S.A.;" tan leather sole with 3-1/2-inch Lucite heel, decorated with rhinestones. $55-65.

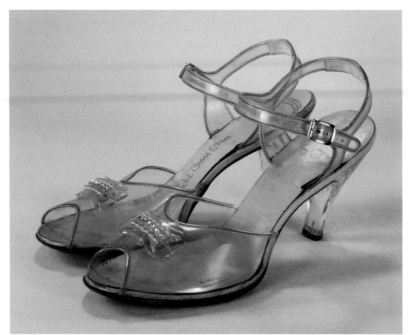

Clear plastic open-toed, ankle-strap sandal, with rhinestone decorations on the vamp; gold stamped on right shoe, "Red Cross Shoes;" tan leather sole with a 2-1/2 inch Lucite heel. $55-60.

Showing the Lucite heel, with a "cut glass" design.

Black suede and clear plastic open-toed, slingback sandal, with a clear plastic, rhinestone decorated bow on the vamp; gold stamped on insoles, "mannequins, the model shoe;" black leather sole with a 3-inch Lucite heel. $55-65.

Clear plastic open-toed, slingback sandal, with a tan leather sole and a 3-inch Lucite heel, showing a "cut glass" design. $55-60.

Clear plastic, open-toed slide, with a "Spring-O-Lator" insole, and a 3-1/2-inch "confetti filled" Lucite heel. $85-90.

Opposite page:
A fuchsia and red silk chiffon gown, with ruffles at the hemline. Worn with a red feather boa, and a rhinestone tiara. Shoes are ivory and silver brocade and clear plastic 1950s slingback sandals, with Lucite heels. *Modeled by Elisa Buratto. The gown, shoes, and boa are from the model's collection. Lisa Leaverton provided the tiara.*

Photograph of slingback sandal, showing the decoration on the vamp and heel.

Ivory and silver brocade fabric and clear plastic open-toed, slingback sandal, decorated with rhinestones; gold stamped on left insole, "Princess ORIGINALS by EDUCATOR," and on the left, "Caprice Feminine Footwear Made in the U.S.A. by Kirsch;" tan leather sole with 4-inch Lucite stiletto heel, also decorated with brocade and rhinestones. *Courtesy of Elisa Buratto.* $95-115.

Green satin open-toed, slingback sandal, with a rhinestone decorated Lucite heel. *Courtesy of DUHCC.* $85-95.

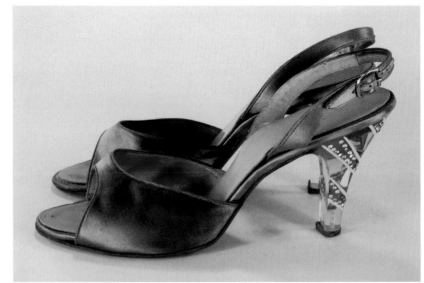

Showing the green satin evening sandal, with the rhinestone decorated heel.

Open-toed, slingback clear plastic sandal, with plastic flowers on the vamp; gold stamped on both floral fabric insoles, "SAKS FIFTH AVENUE, Fenton Last;" tan leather sole with 4-inch stiletto heel. $95-115.

Right:
Gray suede and clear plastic open-toed, slingback sandal; gold stamped on the right insole, "foxy Lady;" tan vinyl sole with 4-inch boulevard heel. $40-45.

Right:
Showing the floral fabric stiletto heels of the clear plastic slingback sandals.

137

Showing the heel of the pink leather slingback sandals.

Pink leather open-toed, slingback sandal, with Dresden china flowers and crystal decoration on the vamp; gold stamped on insoles, "Herbert Levine Fine Shoes, Hand Lasted," and in black ink, the word, "Dresden;" tan leather sole with a 3-inch boulevard heel. $175-225.

Black suede and clear plastic open-toed, slingback sandal; gold stamped on both insoles, "Stanley Philipson;" tan leather sole with a 4-inch boulevard heel. $45-50.

Open-toed, slingback brocade and clear plastic sandal, with a flat fabric bow on the vamp; stamped on insoles, "life stride;" tan vinyl sole with a 4-inch spike heel. $40-45.

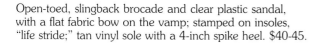

Black suede open-toed, slingback evening sandal, with a bow and a black glass decoration on the vamp; labeled on right insole, "Cameo Shoe Creations;" black leather sole with a 4-inch spike heel. $45-48.

Opposite page:
Black silk late day or "cocktail" dress, with "lattice" detailing around the neckline. Worn with black silk gloves, with beading, and a gray iridescent glass beaded pocketbook. Shoes are 1950s gray iridescent kid open-toed, slingback sandals. *Modeled by Colleen Bergin.* $65-85.

Gray iridescent kid open-toed, slingback sandal, with a gray stone, surrounded with rhinestones on the vamp; gold stamped on the right insole, "french room originals," and on the left, "CHANDLER'S;" black leather sole with 4-inch French heel.

Blue leather slipper, elaborately decorated with glass beads and sequins on the vamp; stamped on the flat leather sole, "Made in Hong Kong, Genuine Leather Sole and Upper." $40-45.

Black suede open-toed evening pump, with a suede strap decoration on the vamp; gold stamped on right insole, "mademoiselle T.M. REG., the fashion shoe," and on the left, "Hess Apparel;" black leather sole with 4-inch spike heel. $48-55.

Black suede open-toed slide, with rhinestone covered "crescent shapes" on the vamp; gold stamped on insoles, "mademoiselle" and "Spring-o-lators;" black leather sole with 4-inch French heel. $85-95.

Black satin slide, decorated with iridescent blue sequins; gold stamped on right insole, "Thos. Cort LTD.," and on left, "SPRING-O-LATOR;" black leather sole with 4-inch spike heel. *Courtesy of Mary Efron.* $95-115.

Black faille slide, with elaborate "lattice work" vamp, and "Spring-o-lator" type insole; gold stamped on right insole, "Mandel's Fascinating Slippers," and on left, "Skyscrapers, New York;" black leather sole with a 4-1/2-inch stiletto heel. $85-95.

Nylon slip in shades of lilac and blue, designed by Emilio Pucci. Shoes are 1950s shiny rose kid slides, with a strap across the instep. *Modeled by Emily Fischer.*

144

Shiny rose kid slide, with a strap across the instep, fastened with a rhinestone decorated buckle; gold stamped on insoles, "DEBONAIRES, Made Expressly for DAVID, Ft. Lauderdale, Hand Lasted;" tan leather sole with 4-inch spike heel. $95-115.

Green silk damask pump; gold stamped on the green silk insoles, "Delman, New York, Paris;" tan leather sole with a 3-1/2-inch stiletto heel. *Courtesy of DUHCC*. $85-95.

Red silk brocade pump; gold stamped on right insole, "Cameo Room Fashions," and on left, "spire toe;" tan leather sole with a 3-1/2-inch stiletto heel. *Courtesy of DUHCC*. $65-85.

View of the green damask pumps, showing the stiletto heels.

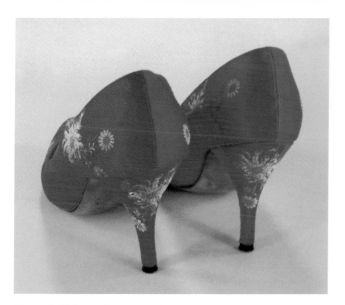

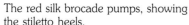

The red silk brocade pumps, showing the stiletto heels.

Black suede open-toed, slingback sandal, with gold metal mesh stripes on the vamp, and an unusual pointed toe; gold stamped on the right insole, "herbert levine," and on the left, "THE BLUM STORE, PHILADELPHIA," black leather sole with a 3-1/4-inch spike heel. $95-115.

Black kid open-toed, slingback sandal, with a kid string bow on the vamp, and an unusual pointed toe; gold stamped on the right insole, "herbert levine," and on the left, "THE BLUM STORE, PHILADEL-PHIA;" black leather sole with a 3-1/4-inch spike heel. $95-115.

Tan burlap wedge-soled mule, decorated on the vamp with a large flower, made of iridescent copper beads; tan leather sole with 3-inch carved wedge-heel. $55-60.

Ivory silk satin robe, lined with rose silk, hand painted in a "Pegasus" motif, additionally decorated with rose colored rhinestones. Shoes are 1950s copper beaded pumps. *Modeled by Marcie Behanna.*

Copper beaded
pump, with layered
beading on vamp;
gold stamped on
insoles, "KUNG
BROS., H. K.
HILTON HOTEL,
HONG KONG;" tan
leather sole with
3-inch spike heel.
$75-85.

Reptile pump, designed with stripes of multi-colored lizard; stamped on right insole, "Genuine Shenanigans Reptile;" tan leather sole with a beige 2 inch Cuban heel. *Courtesy of Matthew Smith.* $45-50.

Gray "textured" leather open-toed, slingback pump, with a black velvet bow with a rhinestone center on the vamp; stamped on the right insole, "PALIZZIO, new york," and on the left, "BOLDRICK'S FINE SHOES, rortora last, hand lasted;" black leather sole with a 3-1/4-inch spike heel. $95-115.

Brown lizard open-toed, slingback sandal; gold stamped on right insole, "Couture HAND LASTED;" tan leather sole with 3-1/2-inch stiletto heel. $45-50.

150

Printed silk open-toed, slingback sandal, in shades of green, tan, and orange; gold stamped on insoles, "SAKS FIFTH AVENUE, Fenton Last;" tan leather sole with a 3-1/2-inch spike heel. $85-95.

Lilac kid open-toed, slingback evening sandal, with leaf and rhinestone decoration on the vamp; gold stamped on right insole, "Queen Quality;" tan leather sole with a 4-inch boulevard heel. $65-75.

Red leather open-toed, ankle-strap sandal, with crossing straps and perforations on the vamp, lined with pale pink kid; gold stamped on insoles, "CUSTOM SHOE MAKING by Anthony Mascioli, NEW YORK;" tan leather sole with a 3-inch modified boulevard heel. $110-115.

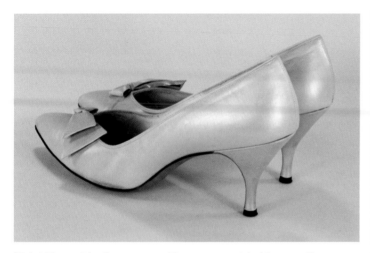

Pink iridescent leather pump, with an asymmetrical bow on the vamp; gold stamped on insoles, "Pacelle SAKS FIFTH AVENUE;" tan leather sole with a 3-inch spike heel. $45-48.

Opposite page:
Charcoal gray and red tweed suit, with a fitted jacket and full skirt. Worn with red nylon gloves, and a red patent leather pocketbook. Shoes are 1950s red patent leather pumps. *Modeled by Marcie Behanna.*

Red patent leather pump, with red leather decoration on vamp, and triangular cut-out; gold stamped on insoles, "The Foot Saver Shoe, and SHORTBACK LAST;" tan leather sole with a 3-inch Continental heel. $28-35.

Red leather pump, with an "open" burgundy leather buckle on the vamp; gold stamped on insoles, "Windsor Fashions;" black leather sole with a 3-1/2-inch spike heel. $48-50.

Iridescent gray leather pump, with a mother-of-pearl buckle on the vamp; gold stamped on right insole, "Macomfort Sock, PAT. PENDING, Minuette Last;" black leather sole with a 3-1/2-inch spike heel. $48-50.

Pale green iridescent leather pump, with decorative "leaves" stitched on the vamp; gold stamped on right insole, "Cameo Room Fashions, UNBREAKABLE HEEL, LIFE LONG LIFT, and on left, "PIN-TOE;" tan leather sole with a 4-inch stiletto heel. $55-60.

Above:
Lilac leather pump, with small leather bow on the vamp; gold stamped on right insole, "custom lasted, DeLiso Debs Bovary," and on left, "Made Expressly for Gimbel Brothers, Philadelphia, DeLiso Debs Bovary;" tan leather sole with 4-inch stiletto heel. $48-55.

Above right:
Iridescent tangerine leather and clear plastic pump, with saw-tooth detailing on the vamp; gold stamped on right insole, "Dino Beautiful Shoes;" tan leather sole with 4-inch stiletto heel. $45-48.

Right:
Black mesh pump, with a black silk bow on the vamp; gold stamped on insoles, "mademoiselle, the fashion shoe, stilettoe PUMP;" black leather sole with a 4-inch stiletto heel. $55-60.

155

Pale blue printed lace kid pump, with decorative tie and perforations on vamp; insoles gold stamped, "SAKS FIFTH AVENUE Fenton Last;" tan leather sole with 3-1/2-inch stiletto heel. $75-85.

Opposite page:
Red silk jersey gown,
designed by Maryjanet
McNamara. Shoes are late
1950s red leather pumps,
with stiletto heels. *Modeled
by Francesca Stewart.*

Open-shank red leather
pump, with a tapered toe;
gold stamped on insoles,
"Quali Craft;" tan vinyl sole
with a 4-1/2-inch stiletto heel.
$40-45.

Brown suede opera pump, with a pointed toe; gold stamped on insoles, "Vive Promette, PATENT PENDING;" tan leather sole with a 4-inch stiletto heel. Opera pumps are actually quite rare. Remember that the upper is cut from one single piece of fabric or leather. $55-60.

Opposite page:
Strapless cotton sundress, floral printed in shades of gold and tangerine on a gray and white ground, with a tangerine silk chiffon drape in back. Shoes are late 1950s printed fabric pumps, with stiletto heels. *Modeled by Jennifer Weigand.*

Printed linen pointed-toe pump, in shades of tangerine, green, and white; illegible markings on insole; tan leather sole with a 4-inch stiletto heel. *Shown with matching clutch style pocketbook.* $45-50.

Open-shank floral fabric pump, with an asymmetrical bow on the vamp, and same fabric insoles; tan leather sole with 4-inch spike heel. $95-110.

Silk print pumps in shades of tan, brown, and green "feathers;" gold stamped on right insole, "mademoiselle T.M. Reg. the fashion shoe," and on left, "hess's, ALLEN-TOWN, PA., Empress Last;" tan leather sole with 3-1/2-inch stiletto heel. $55-65.

Open-shank brown suede pump, with brown velvet ribbon across the vamp; gold stamped on right insole, "DePerini ORIGINALS, GUARANTEED HEEL;" tan leather sole with a 4-inch stiletto heel. $55-65.

Right:
Pale green iridescent woven plastic pump; stamped on right insole, "CUSTOM ORIGINALS, COMBINATION LAST, NARROW HEEL;" tan vinyl sole with a 3-inch stiletto heel. *Shown with matching pocketbook.* $35-40.

Open-shank black suede pump, with a black silk rosette on the vamp; gold stamped on right insole; "andrew geller exquisite footwear," and on left, "FARR'S;" black leather sole with a 4-inch stiletto heel. $75-85.

Black linen pointed toe pump, with red and green linen floral appliqué; gold stamped on insoles, "I. Miller, BEAUTIFUL SHOES;" black leather sole with a 4-inch stiletto heel. *Courtesy of David Sterner.* $95-100.

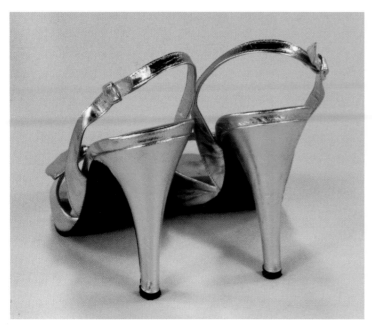

Showing the stiletto heels of the gold kid sandals.

Gold brocade gown with a full-length
matching coat. Shoes are late 1950s gold
kid open-toe, slingback sandals, with stiletto
heels. *Modeled by Francesca Stewart.*

Open-toed, slingback gold kid sandal, with a black leather sole, stamped "Made in Italy," and a 4-1/2-inch stiletto heel. $45-50.

Moss green printed leather pump, with a pointed toe; gold stamped on right insole, "I. Miller Beautiful Shoes," and on left, "Dayton's;" tan leather sole with a 4-inch stiletto heel. *Courtesy of Mary Efron.* $95-125.

Black patent leather pump, with a bow on the vamp, and tapered toe; black leather sole with a 4-inch stiletto heel. $45-50.

Silk print pump in shades of avocado green, burgundy, and blue; gold stamped on insoles, "DeLiso Debs, Designed by Palter DeLiso;" tan leather sole with 3-inch French heel. $45-50.

Rose and gray floral brocade pump, with a pointed toe; gold stamped on insoles, "Palizzio;" tan leather sole with a 4-inch stiletto heel. $75-80.

Pale blue suede and iridescent blue leather pump, with an open-shank and decorative perforations on the vamp; gold stamped on insoles, "troylings, Styled by Seymour Troy, Embassy Last;" tan leather sole, with a 4-inch stiletto heel. $105-115.

Showing the open-shank and stiletto heel.

Green and black striped fabric pump, decorated with a "bunch of grapes" on the vamp; gold stamped on right insole, "Regency," and on left "ALEXANDER'S, NEW YORK-WHITE PLAINS;" black leather sole with a 4-inch stiletto heel. $95-110.

View of the pumps, showing the "bunch of grapes" on the vamp, and the insoles.

Rear view of the stiletto heel, showing the dramatic use of stripes.

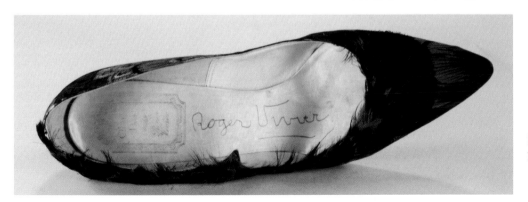

Blue and green printed silk pump, decorated across the vamp and on the outside with dyed-to-match feathers, with a tan leather sole and a 3-3/4-inch stiletto heel; stamped in gold on the ivory satin insole, "Christian Dior Roger Vivier," and additionally signed by his hand in blue ink, "Roger Vivier." No price available. *Courtesy of Liz McGarrity.*

Photograph of the blue and green silk pump, showing Roger Vivier's signature.

Black fabric pump, with a mesh vamp, in a floral motif; gold stamped on insoles, "Styled in France, Bouquet de Paris by Beck;"black leather sole with a 4-inch stiletto heel. $45-50.

Opposite page:
Burgundy wool suit, with jeweled buttons, and three-quarter length sleeves. Worn with white "driving" gloves, and a burgundy leather pocketbook. Shoes are late 1950s burgundy iridescent leather, and rust suede pumps, with stiletto heels. *Modeled by Adria Hadley.*

Burgundy iridescent leather and rust suede pump; right insole gold stamped, "Palizzio...Very New York, cleo last, hand lasted," and the left, "The Smart Shop, Greenville, Miss., cleo last, hand lasted;" tan leather sole with 4-inch stiletto heel. $85-95.

Multi-colored velvet and rhinestone decorated pump, with a 4-inch stiletto heel, pointed toe, and tan leather sole; gold stamped on ivory satin insole, "Delman, New York, Paris." *Courtesy of Liz McGarrity.* $165-185.

Photograph of the multi-colored velvet and rhinestone decorated pump, showing the decoration of the heel.

1960s

The stiletto-heeled pump, with an extremely pointed toe, continued into the early 1960s. Fabric shoes, with matching pocketbooks, were popular for summer. As early as 1962, lower heels became fashionable, and toes became less pointed. By the mid-1960s, the square toe was in fashion, and Roger Vivier and others were designing shoes with open sides or sling-backs and square buckles on the vamps. The heels were getting chunkier as the decade progressed, and those of us who followed the fashion trends were wearing our "Sergeant Pepper" suits with chunky-heeled shoes made of tooled leather, inlaid with metal. Fashion designer Andre Courreges, in the fall if 1963, (*Fairchild's Dictionary of Fashion*, p. 54) introduced a white calf-length, low-heeled fashion boot for wear with miniskirts. Adaptations of this style later became known as "go-go boots," because they were worn by so called "go-go dancers," who entertained at nightclubs. The boots, which were similar to the boots worn by majorettes and cheerleaders since the 1940s, were "trendy" for a short time during the mid-1960s. Imitating boots of the 19th century, "granny boots" gained popularity, especially with the "flower children." These fashion boots were almost knee high, and laced up the front.

White leather pump, with multi-colored leather vamp, in pastel shades; gold stamped on right insole, "troylings," and on left, "HYLANDER'S, WILMINGTON;" tan leather sole with a 3-1/2-inch stiletto heel. $45-50.

Also popular were black, white, and ivory chunky-heeled, tight-fitting vinyl boots, or stocking boots. By the end of the decade, these boots had climbed over the knee!

The market is strong today for 1960s and 1970s shoes, particularly the platforms. Costume designers vie with those planning to attend a "theme" party, or high school reunion, to get their hands on these prizes (platform shoes), which are getting more difficult to find as time goes on.

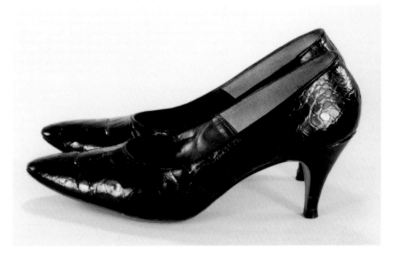

Black alligator pump, with a pointed toe; gold stamped on insoles, "B. Altman & Co., Fifth Avenue, New York, The Balta, REG. U.S. PAT. OFF.;"tan leather sole with a 3-inch spike heel. *Courtesy of DUHCC.* $65-75.

Opposite page:
Leopard velvet wrap coat, with a black plush lining.
Worn over a silk late day or "cocktail" dress. Shoes are
1960s black silk pumps. *Modeled by Elisa Buratto. The
coat, dress, and shoes are from the model's collection.*

Black silk faille pump, with a pointed toe; gold stamped
on right insole, "design by Evins," and on left, "MADE
EXPRESSLY FOR I. MAGNIN & CO.;" black leather
sole with a 3-inch triangular heel. *Courtesy of DUHCC.*
$65-75.

173

Gold lamé wedge-soled mule, decorated with a gold rose and mink fur on the vamp; stamped on insoles, "Nite-Aires;" tan suede sole with a 2-1/2-inch wedge heel. $40-45.

Gold kid ballerina flat or skimmer, with a thin leather sole and a small stacked heel; lined with ivory kid; gold stamped on right insole, "Capezio," and on left insole, "Bonwit Teller." *The author wore these shoes in 1960.* $15-20.

Right:
Mustard yellow suede pump, with a strap across the vamp, and a pointed toe; gold stamped on insoles, "Naturalizer, The Shoe With The Beautiful Fit;" tan leather sole with a 3-inch spike heel. $40-45.

Right:
Silver and white brocade pump, with a pointed toe; gold stamped on both insoles, "Naturalizer, THE SHOE WITH THE BEAUTIFUL FIT, SPECIAL FEATURE Hidden Fit, PATENT PENDING:" tan leather sole with a 2-3/4-inch spike heel. $40-45.

Open-toed, ankle-strap, black patent leather sandal, with a vamp made of "straps;" gold stamped on insoles, "FASHIONS by Mr. Featherlite Styles, KERRYBROOKS;" black leather sole with a 3-1/2-inch boulevard heel. *Courtesy of DUHCC.* $55-65.

Hot pink silk faille pump, with a pointed toe, and a flat bow on the vamp; gold stamped on insoles, "Roger Vivier, Paris;" tan leather sole with a 2-3/4-inch spike heel. *Courtesy of DUHCC.* $95-115.

Gold kid pump, with a pointed toe; tan leather sole with a 3-inch spike heel. *Courtesy of DUHCC.* $45-50.

Black silk satin pump, with a small decorative strap and rhinestone "button" on the vamp; gold stamped on right insole, "Belgian Shoes by Deleusscher of Bruges;" black leather sole with a 2-1/2-inch modified boulevard heel. *Courtesy of DUHCC.* $50-55.

Tangerine linen pump; gold stamped on right insole, "Margaret Jerrold," and on left, "THE BLUM STORE, PHILA-DELPHIA:" tan leather sole with a 3-inch spike heel. *Courtesy of DUHCC.*

Ivory silk faille pump; gold stamped on left insole, "Capobianco Bottier, 32 Faub St Honore, Paris;" tan leather sole with a 3-1/2-inch spike heel. *Courtesy of DUHCC.* $55-65.

Elaborately decorated slide, with aqua glass beads in a floral pattern on a background of iridescent white sequins; black leather sole with a 3-inch spike heel, also elaborately decorated. $95-115.

Elaborately decorated slide, with silver glass beads in a floral pattern on a background of iridescent white sequins, black leather sole with a 3-inch spike heel, also elaborately decorated. $95-115.

White kid and plastic slide, with a small rhinestone decorating the vamp; gold stamped on right insole, "Williams, FASHIONED for fit;" tan vinyl sole with a 3-inch spike heel. $35-40.

Black kid pump, with a square toe; gold stamped on right insole; "Capezios by Capezio, The Dancer's Cobbler Since 1887," and on the left, "French Boot Shop, FBS of New Rochelle;" tan leather sole with 2-1/2-inch spike heel. *Courtesy of DUHCC*. $45-50.

Black patent leather sandal, made up of three straps; gold stamped on right insole, "Capezios by Capezio, The Dancer's Cobbler Since 1887," and on left, "Best Apparel, Seattle;" tan leather sole with a 2-1/2-inch modified boulevard heel. *Courtesy of DUHCC*. $60-65.

Brown alligator pump, with a pointed toe; gold stamped on right insole, "Genuine Alligator, Brandywiners Exclusives;" tan leather sole with a 1-3/4-inch modified Cuban heel. *Courtesy of DUHCC.*

Black patent leather pump, with an open-shank and a bow on the vamp; gold stamped on insoles, "CREATED BY Lanzo, snug heel fit;" black leather sole with a 3-inch stiletto heel. $45-50.

Black leather pump, with tan leather trim and a tie over the instep; gold stamped on right insole, "Ramblers, A Florsheim;" tan leather sole with 1-1/2-inch common sense heel. *Courtesy of DUHCC.*

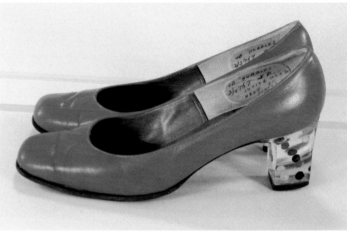

White leather pump, with an open-shank and decorative perforations on the vamp; gold stamped on insoles, "Valentines, THE SOFT APPROACH TO FASHION, VALENCIA LAST;" tan vinyl sole with 2-inch modified baby Louis XV heel. $40-45.

Hot pink leather pump, with a square toe; silver stamped on insoles, "Caprini, elegant fashions for lighthearted feet;" tan leather sole with a 2-inch square Lucite heel, decorated with multi-colored polka-dots. $95-110.

Showing the square Lucite heel.

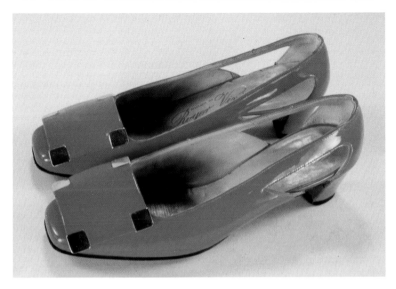

Orange patent leather open-shank pump, with a square toe and brass-edged buckle over the vamp; gold stamped on right shoe, "Designed by Roger Vivier, Paris," and on left, "SAKS FIFTH AVENUE;" tan leather sole, with modified military heel. *Courtesy of Matthew Smith.* $95-115.

Navy blue and burgundy suede pump, with laces over the instep; silver stamped on both insoles, "Mikelos, Athens, Greece;" tan and black leather sole, with a 2-1/2-inch modified boulevard heel. $40-45.

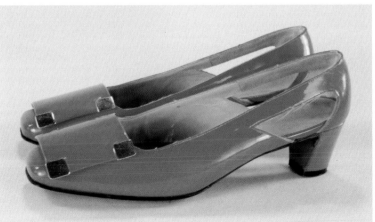

Showing the open-shank and unusual heel of the orange patent leather pumps, designed by Roger Vivier.

White leather pump, appliqued with red leather, on the vamp and across the instep; gold stamped on insoles, "Jakki, ATHENS, GREECE;" tan leather sole with a 2-1/2-inch Louis XV heel. $55-60.

Opposite page:
Pale pink silk satin slacks, with an elaborately beaded blush pink top. The shoes are 1960s ivory satin slingback pumps, elaborately decorated with pearls and rhinestones. *Modeled by Francesca Stewart.*

Showing the elaborately decorated heels and the rhinestone encrusted back-straps.

Ivory satin slingback, square-toed pump, elaborately decorated on the vamp, and around the upper with pearls, rhinestones, and clear glass beads; gold stamped on insoles, "EXCLUSIVE HAND MADE SHOES," tan leather sole with a 2-1/4-inch modified Cuban heel, which is also decorated with pearls and rhinestones. $115-125.

Tan and brown square-toed pump, with three straps across the instep, fastening with buttons; gold stamped on insoles, "Latinas, MADE IN ITALY;" black leather sole with a 2-1/2-inch Louis XV heel. $65-70.

Opposite page:
Floral printed silk mini dress, in shades of blue and purple, with a blue silk coat, with lapels and lining of the same floral printed silk as the dress. Worn with green cotton gloves, a Lucite and brass minaudiere, and purple and pink 1950s glasses. The shoes are 1960s green kid flats, decorated with green kid flowers. *Modeled by Adria Hadley. The dress and coat are from the model's collection.*

Green leather flat, with green leather flowers and cotton leaves decorating the vamp; gold stamped on insoles; "Zodiac Made in U.S.A. by encore;" tan vinyl sole with ½-inch flat heel. $35-40.

Gray leather square-toed pump, with a rhinestone encrusted Lucite "ball" decorating the vamp; gold stamped on insoles, "Arc de Triomphe les beau souliers de dames;" tan leather sole with 2-1/2-inch chunky heel, which is more than half Lucite, encrusted with rhinestones. $175-225.

Yellow leather flat, with yellow leather flowers and cotton leaves decorating the vamp; gold stamped on insoles; "Zodiac Made in U.S.A. by encore," tan vinyl sole with ½-inch flat heel. $35-40.

Below:
Showing the gray leather pumps with a matching pocketbook.

Black patent leather sling-back pump, with brass "fittings" on toe and heel lift, a black leather sole, and a 4-inch "unconventional" heel; gold stamped on beige kid insoles, "PIERRE CARDIN, PARIS." *Courtesy of Liz McGarrity.* $85-95.

The black patent leather pumps, showing the 4-inch heels with brass heel lifts.

Gray suede pump, decorated with black patent leather, and side-laced with black patent leather "ribbon;" gold stamped on insoles, "Made in Spain;" tan leather sole with 3-inch chunky heel. $50-55.

187

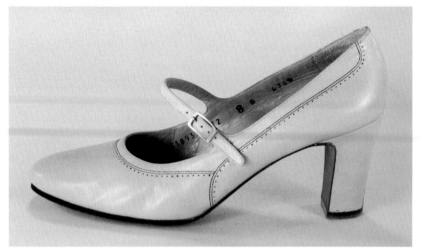

Beige leather pump, with black stitching and perforations decorating the vamp and upper, and a strap across the instep; gold stamped on the right insole; "Salvatore Ferragamo, Florence, Italy," and on the left, "Made for SAKS FIFTH AVENUE;" tan leather sole with a 2-3/4-inch modified boulevard heel. *Courtesy of DUHCC.* $85-95.

Gray and tan leather oxford, with decorative perforations, lined with silver, across vamp and upper; black leather sole with a 2-1/2-inch Cuban heel. *Courtesy of DUHCC.* $45-50.

Black, red, and gold patent leather platform oxford, with a rubber platform and a 3-inch chunky rubber heel; stamped on right insole, "Made in Spain." *Courtesy of Matthew Smith.* $45-50.

Tan and brown suede open-toed, slingback platform sandal, with a rubber platform and a 3-1/2-inch chunky rubber heel; gold stamped on insoles, "Hush Puppies." $30-35.

Tan, beige, and brown suede open-toed, ankle-strap platform sandal; gold stamped on insoles, "SANDLER OF BOSTON;" tan leather sole with a 3-inch chunky heel. $40-45.

189

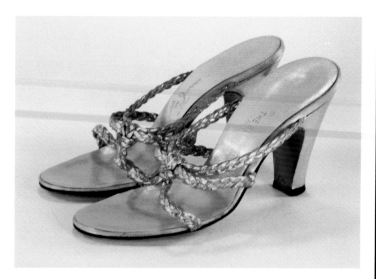

Gold kid slide, with braided straps across the vamp and instep; gold stamped on right insole, "Created by Jerro, NEW YORK," and on left, "THE BLUM STORE, PHILADELPHIA;" tan leather sole with a 3-inch modified French heel. $85-95.

White silk chiffon mini dress, beaded all over with iridescent white glass beads and rhinestones. The shoes are kid slides, with rhinestone-encrusted straps across the vamp and instep. *Modeled by Francesca Stewart.*

190

Silver kid slide, with rhinestone encrusted straps across the vamp and instep; gold stamped on insoles, "Paris Shoes For Women;" tan leather sole with 3-inch spike heel. $95-110.

Black vinyl fashion boot, by Fiorucci, lined with red flannel; molded vinyl sole, imprinted "FIORUCCI, Made in Italy" with a 3-inch French heel. $110-125.

Black stretch body boot. *Modeled by Francesca Stewart.*

Left:
The stocking boot, a fashion boot made of vinyl, leather, or fabric with no zipper, fitting the leg closely like a stocking, developed into the body boot, in the mid-to-late 1960s. First reaching to the thigh, and then with attached panties, the body boot was the height of "mod" fashion. *Modeled by Francesca Stewart.* $75-95.

Dark brown tweed suit, with a belted jacket, and a mini skirt. The boots are dark brown suede knee-high fashion boots, with side zippers. *Modeled by Elisa Buratto. The suit and boots are from the model's collection.* $65-85.

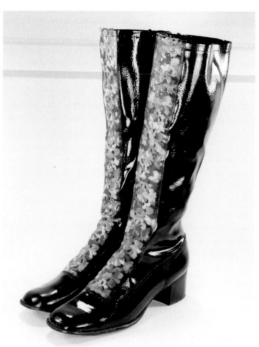

Brown suede and leather knee-high fashion boot, with a side-zipper from the ankle to mid-calf; lined with brown kid; stamped on linings of boots, "Yves Saint Laurent, Paris;" brown leather sole with 3-inch stacked chunky heel. $125-140.

Silk floral print dress and coat, designed by James Galanos. The print is of red roses with pale green leaves on a black ground. The 1960s fashion boots are black vinyl, embroidered with flowers. *Modeled by Marcie Behanna.*

Black stretch vinyl knee-high fashion boot, embroidered with flowers; side-zipper and black ribbed vinyl sole with 2-inch stacked chunky heel. *Courtesy of Matthew Smith.* $125-150.

194

Left:
Leopard print bikini. The 1960s slides are gold kid with straps across the vamp and the instep, decorated with "butterflies" of gold glass beads and pearls. *Modeled by Francesca Stewart.*

Gold kid slide, with straps across the vamp and instep, decorated with a "butterfly" of gold glass beads and pearls; black vinyl sole, labeled "Made in Philippines," with a 2-3/4-inch chunky heel. $55-60.

White kid thong sandal, decorated with a cluster of pink and green beads; tan vinyl sole with a 3-inch chunky heel. $40-45.

Gold leather pump, with stitching and colored rhinestones in various sizes decorating the vamp; gold stamped on right insole, "CALIFORNIA Cobblers, MADE IN THE U.S.A.;" tan vinyl sole with a 1-1/2-inch barrel heel. $30-35.

Red leather T-strap sandal, gold stamped on insoles, "domani, MADE IN ITALY:" tan leather sole with a 1-1/2-inch triangular-shaped brass heel. $45-50.

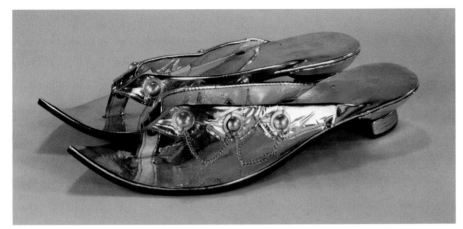

Shiny silver kid slip-on, with silver "circles" and draped chains decorating the straps; tan leather sole with an unusual two-part 1-1/2-inch heel. Possibly Turkish. $40-45.

Silver lamé square-toed, double ankle-strap pump ; the ankle-straps are decorated with rhinestones, and the right insole is stamped, "Fantura;" tan vinyl sole with 1-3/4-inch modified boulevard heel. $40-45.

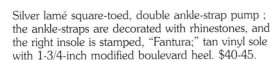

Right:
"The Souper Dress," a Campbell's soup can patterned A-line sleeveless mini-dress, made of printed paper and cellulose. The Andy Warhol Museum owns a duplicate of this dress. The 1960s red leather T-strap "mod" shoes seem to go with the dress. *"The Souper Dress" is from the collection of Lisa Leaverton. Modeled by Francesca Stewart.*

Opposite page:
Red leather T-strap, "mod" Mary Jane, with decorative perforations on the vamp and quarter; gold stamped on insoles, "joyce of California;" tan vinyl sole with 1-1/2-inch chunky heel. $40-42.

Gold and silver lamé mini dress, made in a rib weave, with a front zipper and a mandarin collar. The 1960s shoes are gold lamé "Mary Jane," pumps, with a strap over the instep, and a rhinestone buckle. Worn with lace tights. *Modeled by Marcie Behanna.*

Gold lamé "Mary Jane" pump, with a strap over the instep, and a rhinestone buckle; gold stamped on both insoles, "Continental Fashions by dominic;" tan vinyl sole with a 2-1/4-inch square heel. $40-42.

1970s

Some of the shoe fashions of the 1960s continued into the 1970s, especially the boots, with styles of all descriptions becoming fashionable. Perhaps the most exceptional style, which has never been duplicated, was the over-the-knee suede boot, in an array of colors. However, if any style epitomizes the 1970s, it is the platform shoe. As early as 1970, the platform clog (shoe with thick wooden or cork sole) became popular. During the late 1960s, the "cork-wedge" sandal had appeared, but it was not until the early 1970s that the "cork-platform" appeared. Some of these shoes were surprisingly lightweight, considering that the platform was four or five inches high. Platform shoes became "trendy" for young men by the mid-1970s, and the style was embraced by the "disco-generation." The oxymoron leisure suit was in fashion and with it a few styles of non-traditional shoes for men.

Paisley fabric square-toed pump, in shades of pink, blue, and gold; gold stamped on insoles, "Mijji;" tan leather sole with a 2-1/2-inch boulevard heel. $40-42.

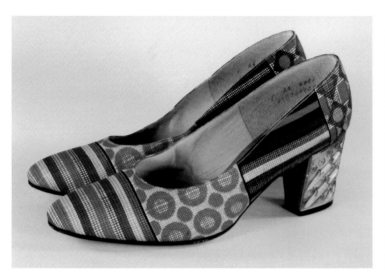

Rear view of the elaborately carved wood heels, which are stylistically compatible with the fabric.

African fabric pump, in shades of tan and blue; gold stamped on insoles, "palizzio;" tan leather sole with an elaborately carved (wood) Cuban heel. $75-85.

Black velvet slingback platform sandal, made of two "lattice work" straps, with tan vinyl sole and 3-inch chunky heel. $40-42.

Gold braid slingback sandal, with a mesh of "braids" making up the vamp; gold stamped on insoles, "Made in Italy;" tan leather sole with a 2-1/2-inch chunky heel, covered in gold kid. $40-45.

Opposite page: Tone-on-tone blue jeans and shirt from the model's wardrobe. The 1970s platform sandals are pale blue suede slingbacks, made up of numerous small straps across the instep. *Modeled by Colleen Bergin.*

Pale blue suede open-toed, slinngback sandal, made up of numerous straps crossing the instep; gold stamped on right insole, "rothman's SHOE SALONS OF FLORIDA," and on left, "Stanley Philipson;" tan leather sole with a 3-1/4-inch square heel. $75-85.

Cotton print mini shift, with a "mod fashion" motif in shades of lilac and green on a white ground. The 1970s sandals have cork wedge heels and platforms, and lilac canvas straps. *Modeled by Francesca Stewart.*

Cork wedge-soled sandal,
with lilac canvas uppers,
made of ankle-straps and a
vamp of braided straps;
vinyl sole with a 4-1/4-inch
cork heel. $40-45.

Rope-covered wedge-soled (wide) ankle-strap sandal, with black satin uppers, trimmed with red and green floral braid; gold stamped on insoles, "chic;" rubber sole with 4-inch wedge heel. $45-50.

Cork wedge-soled slip on, with "round" copper leather straps; gold stamped on insoles, "Quali Craft Casualets;" rubber sole with 4-inch cork wedge heel. $35-40.

Black patent leather open-toed, ankle-strap sandal; gold-stamped on insoles, "Milan Shore Italian Line;" tan leather sole with 4-inch boulevard heel. $45-48.

Left:
White leather and wood grain open-toed, ankle-strap platform sandal; gold stamped on insoles, "Made in Italy;" vinyl sole with a 4-inch chunky heel. $75-85.

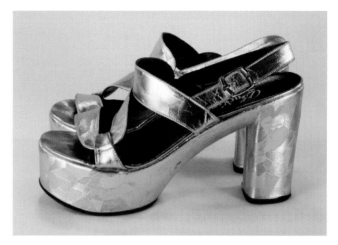

Shiny gold kid open-toed, ankle-strap platform sandal; gold stamped on insoles, "Buckingham;" black leather sole with 4-inch chunky heel. The construction of these platform shoes is unusual. They appear to have been molded, and covered with gold kid. $95-115.

Men's green leather platform oxford, trimmed with yellow kid and laced with striped cotton laces; tan leather sole with 3-inch chunky heel. These shoes were custom made for an entertainer, and are beautifully crafted. *Courtesy of Matthew Smith.* $175-225.

Men's brown and yellow patent leather platform oxford, with decorative perforations on the vamp and across the quarter; gold stamped on insoles, "The Worthmore Shoe, REG. U.S. PAT. OFF;" molded rubber sole with a 3-1/2-inch chunky heel. $95-115.

Men's red leather platform slip-on, with black kid trim; leather soles with 4-inch chunky heel. These shoes were custom made for an entertainer, and are beautifully crafted. *Courtesy of Matthew Smith.* $225-250.

Men's brown leather platform slip-on, with a tassel on the vamp; brown leather sole, and leather covered platform and 4-inch chunky heel. $95-100.

Men's blue leather platform square-toed oxford, with yellow and red kid trim; black leather sole with a 4-inch chunky heel. *These shoes were custom made for an entertainer, and are beautifully crafted. Courtesy of Matthew Smith.* $225-250.

Front view of the blue leather oxfords, showing the red and yellow stripes across the vamp.

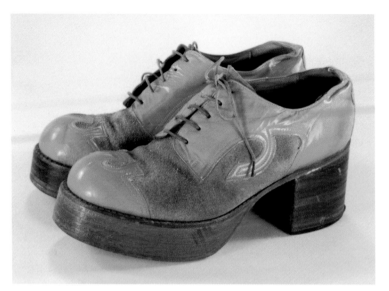

Men's tan leather and moss green suede platform oxford, with a brown leather sole and a 3-inch stacked leather heel. These shoes were custom made for an entertainer, and are beautifully crafted. *Courtesy of Matthew Smith*. $225-250.

Multi-colored glitter ankle-strap platform sandal, with a vamp made of two wide straps; stamped on right insole, "Quali Craft;" molded platform sole, from 2 to 5-inches. *Courtesy of Matthew Smith*. $85-95.

Gold glitter ankle-strap platform sandal, with a vamp made of two wide straps; gold stamped on insoles, "Imperial QUALITY FASHION;" molded platform sole, from 2-1/2 to 4-inches. *Courtesy of Matthew Smith*. $75-85.

Men's black leather platform oxford; with a rubber-coated sole and 3-inch chunky wooden heel, painted with a "city-landscape" of skyscrapers at night. *Courtesy of Matthew Smith.* $225-250.

Rear view of the black leather platform oxfords, showing the skyscrapers painted on the wooden heels.

Blue denim ankle-strap platform sandal, or clog, with embroidery and silver rivets on the vamp; gold stamped on insoles, "De Mura, Made in Italy;" tan vinyl molded sole, from 1 to 3-inches. $40-45.

214

Opposite page:
Navy blue nylon "mod" print mini dress. Worn with a wooden box style "Love" pocketbook, and 1970s platform sandals, made of gold kid. *Modeled by Adria Hadley.*

Gold kid ankle-strap platform sandal, with a vamp made of two wide straps; labeled on insoles, "SHENEL, BAGH, SEPAHSALAR, NO. 121;" tan leather sole with a 4-1/2-inch heel. $115-125.

Above:
Blue velvet slingback platform shoe; gold stamped on insoles, "Tiffany's;" tan vinyl sole with 3-inch chunky heel. $75-85.

Above right:
Tan leather platform slide; gold stamped on insoles, "Nanette Imperials;" tan vinyl sole with 4-inch Spanish heel. $40-45.

Right:
Gold printed plastic slide, with gold kid and beige suede insoles; stamped in blue on insoles, "John Jerro;" tan leather sole with 4-inch spike heel., covered in gold kid. $50-55.

 216

Lucite platform slide, with two ivory patent leather straps; labeled on insoles, "Ginza Exclusive Shoes, Made in Japan;"Lucite sole with rubber attached under the ball of the foot; 4-1/2-inch square Lucite heel. $50-55.

Showing high square Lucite heels.

Red and white leather open-toed, slingback sandal; gold stamped on insoles, "Made in Italy for Quali Craft;"sole of molded red plastic and leather, with a 4-1/4-inch red plastic stiletto heel. $65-75.

Silver kid ankle-strap sandal, with a vamp of numerous narrow kid straps; gold stamped on right insole, "Fiammante by Color Mate;" tan vinyl sole with a 3-1/4-inch modified French heel. $28-30.

Opposite page:
Ivory wool gabardine mini dress, decorated with black soutache and multi-colored large rhinestones. Designed by Todd Oldham. The 1970s slingback sandals are made of thin green kid straps woven together. *Modeled by Colleen Bergin.*

Green kid slingback sandal, made of thin green kid straps woven together; gold stamped on insoles, "Amano, Made in Italy;" tan leather sole with a 3-1/2-inch stiletto heel. $40-45.

White lizard pump, with a tie over the instep; gold stamped on pale pink kid insoles, "John Lobb, LONDON, PARIS, NEW YORK," and various royal seals, as Bootmaker to Queen Elizabeth II, and others; tan leather sole with a 1-1/2-inch common sense heel. *These shoes are beautifully crafted, using the highest quality materials.* $225-250.

Navy blue leather pump, also by John Lobb, with the gold imprints of the various royal seals on the pale gray kid insole; black leather sole with a 2-1/2-inch modified boulevard heel. *These shoes are beautifully crafted, and although the styling is conservative, they would probably last a lifetime!* $95-115.

Red leather ankle-strap, adjustable vamp platform sandal; labeled "Made in Italy by Omnia/c;" molded sole, from 1-1/2 to 2 to 1-1/4 inches; stamped on sole, "patent Omnia/c Made in Italy size 7-37-4." These unusual platform sandals are also roller skates, with a "push-button" on the side of the platform, which releases the wheels of the skates. $275-300.

Side view of the sandal-skates, showing the actual wheels.

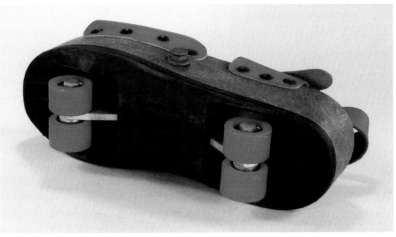

Bottom view of one skate, showing the wheel mechanism.

221

Interview with Howard Davis

The Howard Davis Story
by Liz McGarrity
A Portrait of a Shoe Designer

Howard Davis is a rare individual. Not only did he participate in the heyday of shoe design in New York City in the 1950s and 1960s, he now generously shares his knowledge and expertise with his students at Parsons School of Design in New York City.

Howard was born and raised in Cincinnati, Ohio. His love affair with shoes began when he was a young boy in the 1940s. He took a pair of his oldest sister's "cast off" shoes from the attic, tore them apart, and put them back together in a different, and improved, design. She was upset that he did not ask her permission, but she wore them to a party—and received many compliments. She caught him working on another pair of her shoes, and said: "You better make these look as good as the last ones!" Happy with her second "new" pair of shoes, she gave him a bag of shoes to transform!

After graduating from high school, Howard worked in the display department of an exclusive department store in Cincinnati, called *Jenny*. His fascination with shoes continued, and he began sketching shoes. He became friendly with Edith Booker Thomas, the vice-president of advertising at the store, and showed her his designs. Excited by his talent, she introduced Howard to Herman Delman, who manufactured top-notch shoes worn by celebrities and wealthy women. Three months later, Mrs. Thomas called him into her office, and told him that Mr. Delman had offered him a job in New York. Delman's intention was for Howard to learn the business, from the bottom up. This was an amazing opportunity for an African-American.

Leaving Cincinnati in 1954, Howard came to New York to begin his new career in the stock department of the Delman Shoe Salon at Bergdorf Goodman. He would clean shoes, organize new shipments, and check the accuracy of the codes on the boxes. Often, a selection of shoes was sent out to a celebrity, staying at the Plaza Hotel. When the shoes returned, Howard would place fresh tissue paper in the boxes, and reprint the labels to "freshen them up." He caught glimpses of movie stars shopping at the salon— Barbara Stanwyck, Judy Garland, Pearl Bailey, Lena Horne, Ann Southern, Lana Turner, Ava Gardner, and Paulette Goddard. It was a glamorous experience for a young man from Ohio.

After six months, Howard moved to the factory, located at 345 Hudson Street. Al Fenn, the head of the pattern department supervised and watched over Howard. He learned the different steps of shoe manufacture. The designer would draw his shoe on a wooden shoe form, called a last, "mummified" with paper tape. This would be handed over to the pattern maker, who would cut the paper off the last and create the pattern. The pattern was then given to the cutter, who would cut it out of leather or fabric. These pieces were passed on to the sample maker (also known as the stitcher), who would sew them together. The lasting department would make the shoe, by forming it over a last and attaching a sole. This would be returned to the designer for final adjustments. A fit model would try it on to judge for comfort.

Howard had the great fortune to be working under Roger Vivier, Delman's head designer. Vivier would come to the United States twice a year, from Paris, to supervise the creation of his new designs. Many people consider him to be the ultimate shoe designer of the twentieth century. When Vivier was in town, Howard worked as the sample chaser, handling the last and following it through all the steps previously described. He would then present the finished prototype to the designer.

Delman produced four lines each year: *Spring, Transitional, Fall,* and *Holiday. Spring* and *Fall* were the most important lines, made up of twenty styles. *Transitional* and *Holiday* were usually reworking of the earlier designs in different leathers and fabrics. They had a series of lasts they used over and over again. One last, the "500," was particularly popular and known to fit especially well. Howard learned another important lesson from Ferdinand Ellington, Delman's sketch artist. Ellington advised Howard to perfect his drawing skills, and to learn as much about construction as possible. "This makes for a strong designer," he advised. "No one can tell you that your designs cannot be made."

When Howard first arrived in New York, he lived in Mt. Vernon with Mr. Delman's chauffeur. After a year, he moved to a studio apart-

ment at 132 West 58th Street, close to Bergdorf Goodman. He was attending evening classes at Fashion Industries High School, in shoe design, along with classes in life drawing and perspective at the Art Students League. Meeting artists gave him the opportunity to see another side of creativity, outside the fashion industry. Every evening after dinner, Howard would walk down Fifth Avenue to Saks, then back to Bloomingdales, to study the store windows. He would often get dressed up, and sit in the lobby of the Plaza Hotel to look at the fashionable women. He found inspiration in the lights and costumes of Broadway, and the concerts at Carnegie Hall. He enjoyed a martini at cocktail hour. It was an exciting time!

After Howard had been working at the factory for two and one-half years, Mr. Delman passed away. The company was sold to Genesco, who also owned Jarman, a men's shoe company. It was time for Howard to spread his wings. He left in 1957 to work for Papagallo, for Jean and Mike Bandler. Jean was the designer, and Mike handled production. Papagallo was very well known for a shoe called the "800." It was a kidskin penny loafer, made in a rainbow of colors, and lined with mattress ticking. Another popular style was the skimmer, a ballerina pump with an extreme baby Louis heel, decorated with a bow, and lined with satin. Seasonally, they might replace the bow with a basket of fruit, a leather flower, or a butterfly, to vary the design. Both of these styles were worn by women of all ages. Howard worked as Jean Bandler's assistant for three years. When she left the company, he became the head designer. His years of apprenticeship at Delman served him well. In addition to designing shoes, he made all his own patterns. He learned a new method from Ernest Ferrara, the head pattern maker, using masking tape, instead of brown tape, to "mummify" the last.

At Papagallo, Howard learned more about how the fashion world worked. Jean Bandler took him to fashion shows and to his

Designs by Howard Davis

first Coty Award ceremonies. They would stand on a corner near Bergdorf Goodman and Jean would say: "Out of one-hundred women coming out of the store, you will be lucky if you see five women with fashion sense or taste. Most of the women will look like mannequins in the window." They kept a closet full of shoes for magazines and showrooms to borrow. Howard's designs received a great deal of exposure this way. Papagallo employed many young people, and Howard found a creative, festive atmosphere there. He had keys to the factory at 18th Street and Fifth Avenue, and he worked on the weekends because he loved it so much. Papagallo put out three lines a year—*Spring, Fall*, and *Holiday*. The company would purchase exotic leathers from Fleming Jaffee. They sold ostrich, sharkskin, alligator, lizard, tooled leather, and a painted snakeskin, called "sequin serpent." Howard described their showroom: "It was like a mini-jungle or zoo. As you came off the elevator, there was a huge picture window with snakes behind it. The furniture was covered with leopard skin, and we sat on stools made out of elephant's feet."

When Jean Bandler returned to the company in 1966, Howard felt it was time for him to move on. He worked for a year at Andrew Geller, for their label called "Gamins." His office, along with several other major shoe companies, was located in the Marbridge Building.

In 1967, Howard left Andrew Geller and the shoe business. The nature of the business was changing, partly due to rising labor costs. Shoes were being manufactured offshore, because it was cheaper. Rather than employing designers, some companies were going to Italian factories and choosing existing designs, and simply having their labels put into the shoes. Another innovation was the creation of the "line builder," who oversaw the development of the line. He or she studied the trends, and was in charge of production and marketing. The designer now reported to the "line builder," and was no longer the most important person in the process.

BOOT and SHOE

RECORDER

SEPTEMBER 15, 1962

THE MERCHANDISING GUIDE OF THE INDUSTRY

The Young Influentials

Howard Davis at left.

225

Howard remained in the fashion business and became Vice-President of Design for New Breed Industries. Along with manufacturing Afro-centric clothing, the company published a newspaper and owned a restaurant. He supervised three designers in New York, and four in Los Angeles. The clothing was sold at Macy's, J. C. Penney, Bloomingdales, and Sears. Through this company, Howard met Robert Downey, Muhammad Ali, and Sammy Davis, Jr.—working with them all to design clothes and shoes. The company was an interesting experiment, which ultimately ended after four years. During this period Howard had moved to Harlem, to live in the community for which he was designing clothing. He continued to design clothing for various companies until 1976.

His romance with shoes began again. Howard became a freelance designer for Converse Sneakers, the Sullivan Shoe Company, and Little Falls Footwear. In 1979, he founded his own corporation, called "8 Track." As a research and development company, his goal was to "make comfort beautiful." He was responding to a call from consumers for attractive, comfortable shoes. Working with manufacturers, Howard designed an air-based outsole, and patented an elastic shank. The soles are based on the technology and science of weight distribution, and move weight from the ball of the foot to the outer edge of the shoe. These innovations were used to create shoes that were easy to wear, as well as stylish. Over the last twenty years, Howard has worked to satisfy the needs of the "Baby Boomers," and their children, the "Eco Boomers." Born into "softies" or sneakers, comfort is a first requirement of this generation. Using his soles, both Cobbie Cuddlers and Easy Spirit have each sold over two million pairs of shoes. In 1984, he also designed shoes for Michael Jackson's *Pepsi Cola* concert tour.

Howard has been teaching at Parson's School of Design in New York City for ten years. The class covers all aspects of shoe design

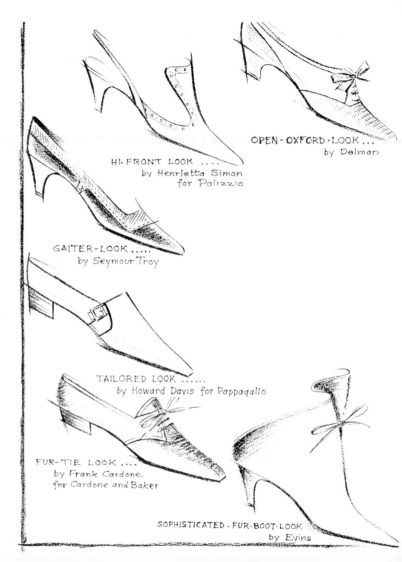

HI-FRONT LOOK ....
by Henrietta Simon
for Palizzio

OPEN-OXFORD-LOOK ...
by Delman

GAITER-LOOK.....
by Seymour Troy

TAILORED LOOK ......
by Howard Davis for Pappagallo

FUR-TIE LOOK ....
by Frank Cardone
for Cardone and Baker

SOPHISTICATED-FUR-BOOT-LOOK
by Evins

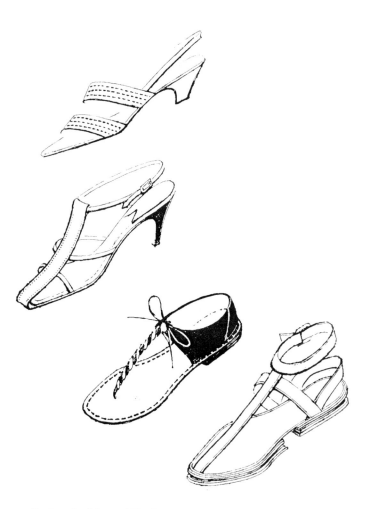

and construction. He tells his students: "Keep your ears open, and be aware of all things—Wall Street, the arts, and current events. These things will find their way inside, and become your inspiration." As a teacher, Howard finds his way inside his students, and inspires. Former students now work for Charles Jourdan, Christian Dior, Coach, American Eagle, Diane Von Furstenburg, Nike, Reebok, Kenneth Cole, Sam & Libby, Calvin Klein, Fila, Donna Karan, 9 West, Converse, Bass, Timberland, Joan and David, Tommy Hilfiger, and the Gap.

Howard Davis is an important figure in the history of American shoe design, and he continues to influence and innovate into the new millennium.

The Interview

Author's note: Liz McGarrity, an artist and costume designer in New York City, interviews Howard Davis, asking the author's questions which are designed to provide an inside look at the shoe industry. His answers reveal a perspective that was gained only through his insight and experience, and willingness to share his ideas with the public. The interview also provides an interesting link between vintage and contemporary footwear.

What inspired you to design women's shoes?
The way the high heel sounded on the street—click, click. The way the shoe makes women walk—more gracefully. I always think of Marilyn Monroe, running next to the train in "Some Like It Hot." Sexy! The way the curve of the heel looked…The way the shoe was decorated.

Designs by Howard Davis

What are the three most important elements of shoe design?

Construction is important. The better the shoe, the longer it lasts. Good construction makes a valuable product. Fit equals comfort. Cosmetics are the third important element—the color of the leather, look of the last, and the heel shape. For the "new age" generation coming along, comfort is the most important thing, because it is associated with lifestyle, health food, and exercise. Comfort did not mean that much twenty years ago. The decade of the 1980s was about glamour. Men were always concerned about comfort. Now they are more open to style.

What are the basic steps in the manufacture of a shoe?

The first step is *designing,* which means sketching and making a pullover (prototype sample attached to a light bass wood last). This is three dimensional, instead of a flat sketch. The next step is *pattern making.* The third step is *lasting.* The upper is attached to a last, and formed into a shoe, incorporating an inner sole, counter, toe box, shank, heel, and sole. The final step is *fitting and finishing,* which involves trial testing of the fit, cleaning, polishing, and touch-up.

Is there any culture/country best known for its contribution to the art and manufacture of shoes?

Yes, Italy. It has a great tradition of shoemaking, and the best leathers. Italy is known for its leather tanning.

Are vintage shoes better made than contemporary shoes?

No. The simple reason is that vintage shoes were sold more for cosmetics, while contemporary shoes are made for comfort. Some of the vintage shoes are better made. In the 1950s factories were making five hundred pairs of shoes a day. Now factories are making several thousand pairs a day—so quality suffers.

In terms of style, why are men's shoes so traditional, and women's shoes so diverse?

Howard Davis

Men are slower to accept change than women. Men's focus on fashion is much narrower than women's. Women are more experimental. Men were always concerned about comfort. Now they are more open to style.

Do women buy more shoes than men? Why?

Yes, the extent of their wardrobe is larger. Having a more extensive wardrobe than men, women like to have shoes to match with all their outfits. They like different colors, different heels, and different decorations. Men have more conservative clothing, and one pair of black shoes and one pair of brown shoes.

What is the best advice you could give a beginning shoe collector?

Look for unusual shoes of any period. It's good to have examples from every decade. The 1920s, '30s, and '40s were the high glamour period. Examples by Vivier, Ferragamo, Perugia, Herbert Levine, and Margaret Jerrold are at the top of the list. They revolutionized shoe design. The Joan Crawford platform, with an ankle strap, is a great silhouette. Contemporary designers to collect are Prada, Manolo Blanick, Andrea Pfister, Jimmy Choo, Christian Laboutian, John Fluevog, Stephane Kellian, Clergerie, and Joan & David.

What are the latest trends in shoe design?

An athletic and casual combination in design is setting the pace today. Trends are caused by the economic situation of the world, music, movies, celebrities, and a grass roots influence from the street. Right now, the heaviest trend setting influence is hip-hop and rap. It is what goes on in the world that dictates what fashion is about—people, places, and things.

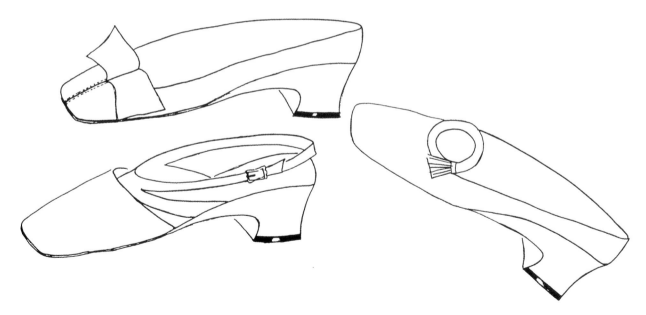

Designs by Howard Davis

229

Styles, such as the platform, seem to reappear. Are there any completely "new" shoes, in terms of style? Do designers get inspiration from vintage shoes?

Prada is creating "new shoes." Their shoes are athletic and casual combined. Yes, designers get inspiration from the past. They do their research work, backtrack, and then try to make it current and utilitarian. They look in the libraries and museums for inspiration.

What are the two most popular, for all time, styles for women?

The basic pump, and the loafer. Both of these styles have existed throughout all the decades of the 20th century.

What do you think about the vintage printed silk, linen, and other fabric shoes? Are fabric shoes more difficult to make than leather?

Fabric shoes are attractive, but limited. It is a seasonal shoe, except satin for eveningwear. Espadrilles are the strongest fabric shoes. They are all difficult to keep clean. They are more difficult to make, because leather stretches, and fabric doesn't. The uppers must be cut at least one-half to one size bigger. Leather can be cleaned during the construction process, not fabric. There is the additional worry that the glue will bleed through the fabric.

Are high heeled shoes for women as popular today as they were in the 1950s?

What dictates the heel height is what's happening in fashion. High heels are not as popular today, because everyone is concentrating on comfort and athletic shoes. It's a smaller number of women (younger, in their twenties) that heels still appeal to. In the 1950s women had no choice. When a woman went out, it was taken for granted that she had heels on. It was a dress code. Now, the consumer makes her own decision. The retailers and fashion magazines no longer dictate to the consumer. The "Baby Boomer" has revolutionized the relationship between the retailer and the consumer.

Liz McGarrity

230

Has the popularity of the sneaker had an effect on the sale of women's fashion shoes?

Absolutely. They became popular because of utility and comfort. They were used at aerobic workouts, and then became fashionable when Reebok started making them in colors. Women became "switch-hitters," wearing sneakers to work, and then changing in the office. People want to emulate athletic celebrities. Sneakers are also very compatible with stretch clothing. If clothes stretch, shoes cannot be far behind! Clothes have to move "like a second skin," so do shoes. Shoes have to go hand in hand with more freedom in clothes. A woman, who used to buy two or three pairs of dress shoes, will buy one pair of dress shoes and one pair of athletic. Why have a wardrobe full of shoes you are not comfortable wearing? Women will get dressed up and wear sneakers with their outfits. Rich women, of the "carriage trade," are now buying the majority of dress shoes, because they won't be walking anyway. They'll be riding in limousines or taxicabs.

Who is/was your all time favorite designer? Why?

Ferragamo. He was a technician. He knew how to combine fashion and technology into one. He revolutionized many things in the footwear industry. He experimented with various materials—plant, fabric, plastic, metal, and cork.

Is it difficult to make a living as an accessories designer? Do most shoe designers work free lance, or independently, or do they work for others?

In the past, companies traditionally had "in house" designers. There are still some of those positions, and those people make the most money now. However, today we see more freelance designers, because companies are able to avoid paying benefits, while getting the same result from the designer. Working freelance does allow you to work for various companies, as long as they are not competitive—street shoes, slippers, athletic shoes. A designer now has to work under a "line builder," when previously he or she had complete control over the line.

How much of the shoe manufacturing today is done in the United States, compared with fifty years ago? Why?

Fifty years ago it was one-hundred percent manufactured in the United States. Now, it is ten percent or less. Starting the in 1960s, because of organized labor, it became too expensive to manufacture shoes in the United States. Although I am pro-organized labor, because it protects the "little guy," I also believe that labor needs to "compromise" more with the owners. Some companies are trying to bring back manufacturing to the United States. I believe this will work if it's done with a modular manufacturing system.

If a person is passionate about becoming a shoe designer, where should she/he study? And then what?

Of course, he or she should study at Parson's School of Design in New York City. Outside of the United States, there is Arsetoria in Italy, and the Cordwainers College in England. These are the most well known schools (in Europe), and accept students from the United States. After his or her courses, a student should develop a portfolio for job hunting, and contact shoe manufacturers themselves. There is an agency, called "Revere," that helps fill all positions in the shoe industry. A student can "intern" while still in school, then look for a job as an assistant designer.

Describe the concept "handmade" in relation to shoes. Are many shoes "handmade"?

A handmade shoe is made almost entirely by hand. The pattern is handmade, and the leather is cut by hand. A person operating the sewing machine sews the shoe. A skiving machine, controlled by a person, thins the leather. The shoe is lasted, pulled, and glued by hand. The finishing and trimming are done by hand. A manufactured shoe starts off with a handmade pattern, but the upper is dye cut, and stitching can be computerized. Machine—separate ones for the toe, the side, and the heel do the gluing and lasting. The finishing and trimming of the outsole is done by machine. Not too many shoes are handmade today, because it is too expensive and time consuming.

What is the most difficult part of the shoemaking process? Why?

The most difficult part is making the "right" style, that the consumer will buy. It is the most horrendous part. It is difficult because no one has a crystal ball! Knowing what the consumer wants can make or break a company. It is difficult to predict what the consumer wants. You have to watch everything—politics, theater. Style has to complement the consumer's life style. Also, you must understand what your factory can produce. That's tough!

Why is the "last" of the shoe often singled out as special?

I always attribute this to romanticism. The "last" becomes almost like your child, especially if it's making money for you. It is more easily identified by a name than a number. It makes it easy for consumers to identify that this is a type of shoe that fit them before.

Are there any retailers (stores) especially well known for their shoes?

Nordstrom department stores are noted for shoes, even in the shoe industry.

How has the computer affected the shoe industry?

I like the computer. It is very helpful for the designer, because you can see changes in color combination, heel height, trimming, and detail—in seconds by pushing a button. In the manufacturing end, it is important for the relationship with the retailer, because it can keep track of inventory very efficiently.

How are boots and slippers different from shoes?

Boots are a seasonal item. Some people consider it fashionable to wear boots all year round, but even if boots fall out of fashion, they will be popular seasonally because of their utility. Boots are above the ankle or above the knee. They use more leather, and are more expensive to make. There is a special last for boots, and the design of the top has to be adjusted for bending the leg.

Slippers are different from shoes in the way they are put together. A slipper is stitched and turned, and different materials are used in its manufacture. A slipper is often washable, can be packed easily, and the construction is lighter than a shoe.

What is the best way to preserve vintage shoes?

Mink oil, felt or tissue, and plastic boxes are the three most important things for preserving vintage shoes. I would rub mink oil into the leather, and do it often, to prevent the leather from drying out. I have little felt bags to keep the shoes in for storage. I keep the shoes in plastic boxes, rather than cardboard. It's better protection.

What is special about the shoe as a fashion accessory?

It is the most important part of the wardrobe. The shoe is the only accessory that has to carry the whole body. It is protecting the feet. Whatever decoration is put on the shoe, defines what that shoe will do. A lug sole protects the foot; a thong shoe is open for a hot climate. The cosmetics define where a shoe is going to take you—a satin shoe to the opera; a lug sole is for climbing a mountain.

Approximately how many pairs of shoes do most people own?

I own twelve pairs of shoes. If we are talking about women, are we comparing them to Imelda Marcos? I think that most women, if they are crazy about shoes, easily have one hundred pairs of shoes. Most women would not have fewer than fifty pairs; most men would not have fewer than five pairs.

What about synthetic materials and the shoe industry. Is leather becoming obsolete? What about heels made of a layer of leather over plastic?

Synthetic materials came into general use in the fashion industry during the 1960s. That is when we first saw plastic belts, vests, jewelry, and shoes. Plastics come in a wide range of colors and yardage, not skins, like leather. Leather is more expensive. Fashion politics also made plastic more acceptable because of the idea that you were not killing animals. The downside of plastic is that is does not stretch, while leather stretches and "breaths." It is possible to go into the shoe business with less money, due to the lower cost of synthetic materials. During the 1960s manufacturers began to mold soles, rather than cut them from leather. This was less expensive.

Plastic heels are also made in a mold. They do not split and warp, as wooden heels, which are made on a lathe. Plastic is cheaper and faster to make. They don't make stacked heels anymore, because it is expensive and heavy. When they got wet, the stack would warp and separate. They would score the leather cover on a plastic heel, to make it look stacked.

Preservation

As a collector, I would put about one hundred years of footwear on a display shelf. I would put the fragile shoes inside cases, away from sunlight and dust, and preserve them so that future generations could enjoy them as much as present and past generations. My suggestions for preservation are based on practical experience.

I remember that when I was a little girl, my father spent one day each year treating all his leather suitcases and belts with saddle soap. He would work the saddle soap into the leather in small circular motions with a damp sponge, let it dry, and buff it slightly. This was a ritual that he observed, like clockwork. I also watched him cleaning and waxing his shoes, as often as once a week. I have seen my husband pay such attention to his shoes.

I don't believe that I really became interested in the care of my own shoes until I began to collect vintage footwear. I have seen rodent damage (the little creatures will eat the leather), moisture damage (from damp basements and mold), heat damage (silk shredded while stored in attics), sun damage (the back of the shoe faded from exposure to sun from a window), and the ravages of dust (shoes sitting on the floor of the closet).

Sometimes the leather appears to be dry. Moisturize leather soles and "uppers" regularly. Schedule a regular time to evaluate the shoes in your collection, and moisturize as needed. After ex-

Small tooled leather box, shaped like a shoe. $300-350.

perimenting with several products, I found that I particularly like to use "Leather Care Lotion" by Etienne-Aigner to moisturize the leather, including the leather sole. If the sole is dyed black and scuffed, I use scuff coating (Kiwi "Scuff Magic" is a good choice) to cover the marks.

I have noticed that shoes which had been thrown into a box with a bunch of other shoes (a presentation which is most often associated with estate sales) are usually out of shape, with sides "caved in," or backs pressed down. If the shoe is permitted to "collapse," the lines created in the leather or fabric will soon crack. It is obvious to me that the best way to preserve a shoe is to stuff it with tissue paper to keep its shape. Use tissue paper to "puff out" your shoes, but do not "over-stuff" them with paper. This is especially important with the antique shoes. Some shoes actually come with

Small hand carved and decorated shoes. $150-175.

little velvet "toe pillows," which give definition to the vamp of the shoe; others come with shoe stretchers, which tend to be harmful to the shoe, causing too much pressure on the sole, even causing it to crack.

A plastic bag around a shoe is usually not a disaster, but there is a chance that moisture will get into the bag and damage the finish on the shoe, or that the bag will "melt" onto the shoe. Shoe designer Howard Davis offered excellent advice when he suggested keeping the shoes in felt bags and plastic boxes, which are available for a reasonable cost at many "dollar stores" and large pharmacies. He also mentioned tissue paper, which shoe stores have traditionally used to separate shoes, so that they do not touch each other, possibly creating damage. Store your shoes somewhere other than in the dry attic or damp basement.

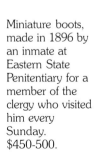

Miniature boots, made in 1896 by an inmate at Eastern State Penitentiary for a member of the clergy who visited him every Sunday. $450-500.

Leg forms used for store display in the 1940s. $10-12 each.

235

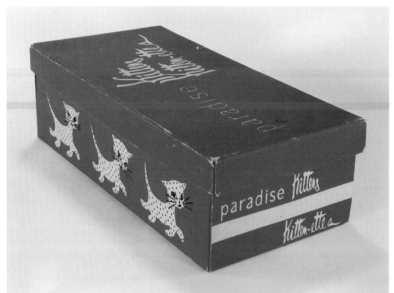

A cheerful shoe box!

A store known for its great shoes!

236

The author's favorite shoe designer!

One of the author's favorite shoe designers!

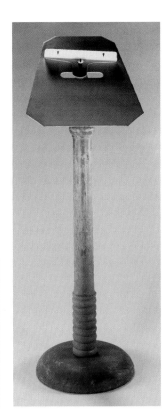

A shoe display stand from the 1920s. $30-35.

237

Footwear Glossary

Fashion has its own language. Here are footwear terms, which may be unfamiliar to the reader, and illustrations that clearly explain shoe language. Two books were particularly useful in the preparation of this glossary: *Fairchild's Dictionary of Fashion*, 2ⁿᵈ Edition, by Charlotte Mankey Calasibetta, Ph.D., (New York: Fairchild Publications, 1988), and *A Dictionary of Costume and Fashion: Historic and Modern*, by Mary Brooks Picken, (Mineola, New York: Dover Publications, Inc. 1957; unabridged republication, 1999). Both are scholarly and informative, and are highly recommended for accurate, concise definitions relating to antique and vintage clothing and accessories.

acrobatic. Soft, lightweight shoes, with buckskin soles, used for gymnastics.

aerobic. Laced shoe of nylon mesh with suede outside counter, toe band, and trim. Usually higher cut than a sneaker, with a shock absorbing mid-sole and a non-skid rubber sole.

alaska. Overshoe with rubberized cloth top, and rubber sole.

ankle-strap. Type of shoe, often a sandal, having a strap attached at the top of the heel that goes around the ankle. Frequently has a **platform** sole.

Arctics. Waterproof rubber boot worn over regular shoes usually with zipper closing, popular in 1940s, revived in 1970s. Also called **galosh.**

baby doll. Shoe, which has a short, wide toe, rounded as in a doll's shoe.

baby Louis heel. Heel like Louis XV heel in shape, but lower in height.

back-strap. Women's open-heeled slipper held on by a heel strap, **sling pump** or **slingback.**

ball heel. Spherical heel made of wood or Lucite, popular since 1960s.

ballerina. Shoe designed to look like a dancing slipper, but having a leather sole and heel lift; a tie string at top can be adjusted for fit.

ballet slipper. Heel-less, plain slipper worn by ballet dancers, usually of satin or lightweight kid, with or without reinforced soles and special toe boxing. Usually tied on around ankle with satin ribbon. Also adapted for street wear.

balmoral. An ankle high shoe, which is laced up the front, not adjusted by buttons or buckles. Called "bal" for short.

barefoot sandal. Low cut, backless shoe with an open vamp and shank; usually fastens with buckled straps.

barrel heel. Heel of nearly cylindrical shape, somewhat resembling a barrel in silhouette.

Bass Weejun. Trademark of G. H. Bass & Co., a division of Chesebrough Pond's, Inc., for a high-quality moccasin-type loafer. Popular with the "Baby Boomers," this shoe has used the same last since 1936.

batt or bat. Shoe for women, which is heavy and low and has laces in front. Worn first in England, it was sent to the colonies in 1636.

Beatle boot. Ankle-high boot with pointed toe and side gores of elastic-styled for men. Probably the first fashionable ankle-high shoe to be worn by men for general wear in place of oxfords since the World War I period. Introduced in the 1960s by the Beatles, an avant-garde rock-music group from Liverpool, England. Also called **Chelsea boot**.

bedroom slipper. Soft, comfortable slipper with flexible sole and usually low heel or no heel. Usually made of felt, soft cotton fabric, or leather.

bell bottom heel. Chunky medium heel, curved inward and then flaring at the bottom, an exaggerated version of a Louis heel.

bicycle bal. Shoe which is laced far down to the toe, and has a protective toecap, and leather circles over the ankle joint. First designed for bicycling, but has been used for other outdoor sports.

Blake. Shoe made by sole-stitching method invented by Lyman Blake. *See McKay*.

block heel. Straight heel similar to Cuban heel, but set further back and approximately the same width at top and base.

body boot. Women's long, tight-fitting boot, reaching to the thigh. Introduced in the late 1960s.

boot. Footwear extending above the ankle. In America, boot usually means top boot, extending well up calf of leg or higher. In England, boot means high cut shoe, as distinguished from slipper, pump, or oxford.

boot blow-up. Plastic or rubber boot form inserted to retain shape when boots are not being worn.

boot stretcher. Form inserted into boot to retain its shape when not being worn, *similar to boot blow up*.

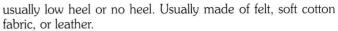

Boot stretchers from the 1960s. $25-28.

239

Little red **booties** from the 1930s. $30-35.

bootee. Boot having short leg. For men, usually made with elastic gore over ankle, or laced front. For infants, usually knitted and tiny.

bootekin. Small boot, variously decorated, usually fancy.

bootie. Short boot made of soft kid, cloth, or wool, worn by infants.

bootikin. Small boot.

bottine. Small boot of fine quality for women; half or low boot.

boudoir slipper. A soft lightweight slipper, with or without a heel, sometimes colorful or richly decorated.

boulevard heel. High, covered wooden heel, similar to Cuban, but more shapely and lighter looking.

bracelet tie. Shoe, often a pump, with ankle strap or straps attached to an extended back piece.

brogan. Heavy pegged or nailed shoe, usually ankle-high, worn by workmen, This shoe is sometimes confused with **brogue.**

brogue. Heavy, sturdy, low-heeled oxford trimmed with perfora-

tions, stitching, and pinking. Originally this was a heel less shoe, of untanned hide with hair left on, which was worn in Ireland and Scottish Highlands.

built-up heel. Leather heel composed of separate pieces of sole leather, or lifts, applied separately and fastened together.

buskin. Women's modern low-cut shoe with elastic goring at instep. Originally (classified as a boot) it extended halfway to knees, was laced with cord or ribbon, and was worn in ancient Greece, chiefly by actors.

carriage boot. Lined boot, usually of fabric, often fur-trimmed. Worn by women in winter over ordinary shoes or slippers, as protection against weather. Originally worn only in carriages to keep the feet warm; later in automobiles; more recently on the street. Some carriage boots are made large enough for both feet to slip into.

cavalier boot. High, soft leather boot with flaring top, as worn with 17th century cavalier costume.

chunky heel. High or medium heel that has exaggerated width—a shoe fad of late 1960s and early 1970s, that returned in the late 1990s.

clog. Shoe, usually of sandal type, having wood or cork sole.

cobcab. Type of clog shoe, worn by women in Orient.

colonial. Low-cut shoe having broad tongue outside, extending above the instep, with large, ornamental buckle. Worn in colonial America, often without tongue.

common-sense heel. Low heel having a broad base. So called because of support it gives and supposed greater comfort.

congress gaiter. Ankle-high shoe having leather or cloth top, often to match costume; adjusted to ankle by elastic gusset at sides, instead of by laces or buttons. Popular in the late 19th century. Also called **congress boot**.

Continental heel. High heel with straight front and slightly shaped back, narrower at the base than the French heel.

cordwainer. Shoemaker. Originally, worker in cordwain or cordovan leather.

cothurnus boot. Half boot, especially one with thick soles, worn by ancient Greeks and Romans as part of theatrical costume.

counter. Piece of stiffened material cut by pattern measurements and used in shoe construction to keep back part in shape. Pasted between lining and outside leather of the quarter. Made of leather of good quality in better shoes; made of fiber or poor leather stiffened with glue in cheaper shoes.

Courreges boot. White calf-length low-heeled fashion boot introduced by French designer, Andre Courreges, in fall of 1963 for wear with miniskirts.

cowboy boot. Boot with high, fancy top, usually decorated with stitching. This type of boot has a Cuban heel, to prevent the boot from slipping from the stirrup when riding horseback.

crepida boot. Ancient Roman low, half-boot with toes uncovered.

crooked shoe. Shoes that distinguish between left and right; first introduced in volume about 1850. Shoes previously were straight and fitted either foot.

Cuban heel. Medium, rather straight heel, without curve of French heel; somewhat narrower at base than flat heel; often of leather.

cube heel. Square-backed heel made of leather or Lucite.

dainty boot. From 1820s to 1880s ankle-high boots worn outdoors by women and children.

demi-boot. Short boot, reaching just to the ankle. Also called **half-boot**.

D'Orsay. Pump-shaped slipper, low-cut at sides in curves extending to the shank of slipper.

draped heel. Heel bound to foot with kerchief-like drapery covering top of heel and back of foot and tied around ankle.

dress. Shoe appropriate for wear with formal dress on social occasions.

Dutch boy heel. Heel similar in shape to that on a Dutch wooden shoe, slanting toward the base. Bottom sometimes shaped like a raindrop.

Elevator shoe. Trade name for men's shoe which increases height by a raised innersole.

espadrille. Rope-soled shoe with strap or canvas upper. Used as bathing shoe.

evening. Women's lightweight decorative slipper or sandal of fabric or leather for wear with evening dress.

fashion boot. Boots not intended for utility, such as hunting, mountain climbing, etc., intended to be worn indoors and out, in place of shoes. Made as a fashion item and not intended to be waterproof. Made in all lengths and fabrics during mid-to-late 1960s and early 1970s. Style is stressed rather than utility.

finnesko boot. Boots made from tanned skin of reindeer and worn with fur side out. Worn by Arctic travelers. Also spelled *finnsko*.

flange heel. Heel flaring outward at bottom to make a wide base.

flat/flattties. Any shoe with broad low heels, or heel-less, worn by children and women for street or eveningwear.

flat heel. Broad, low heel, only slightly shaped at back, usually of leather.

foot measure. Instrument similar to a ruler, for measuring the foot and determining shoe size.

Franco-Cuban heel. Narrow Cuban heel.

French fall. Leather boots with high top wide enough to crush down. Worn in colonial America.

French heel. Curved high heel. Usually made of wood covered

Wooden **foot measure**.

with leather, having thickness of sole leather; or of wood, with leather top lift at bottom. Sometimes made entirely of leather.

gaiter. Ankle-high shoe, buttoned or having elastic sides; originally with cloth top.

golf. Oxford-style shoe made of oil-treated leather, usually given a water-repellent finish, and having foam cushioned innersole. Popularized in the 1920s in two-toned black and white style.

go-go boot. Calf-length white boot, similar to Courreges boot. Named because "go-go" dancers wore it.

granny boot. Women's boots laced up the front in imitation of high-topped shoes of the 19th century.

Grecian sandal. Flat-soled footwear of ancient Greeks, with varying types of strap fastenings. Adapted for evening and play shoes in recent times.

Folding wooden **foot measure**. $45-55.

Harlow pump. Sabot-strap pump with high chunky heel popular in the early 1970s. Named after shoes worn by Jean Harlow, Hollywood actress of the 1920s and 1930s.

Harlow slipper. Boudoir slipper, similar to toeless slides with medium to high heel, trimmed with marabou. Copied from slippers worn by Jean Harlow, the Hollywood actress, in the late 1920s and 1930s.

heel. Piece beneath back part of shoe, boot, or other foot covering; made of leather, rubber, wood, metal, etc. varying in shape and height. Height measured vertically, at side, just back of heel breast, from top lift to upper edge of sole, in eighths of inch.

heel breast. Forward face of heel on shoe.

heel lift. One of separate pieces, or layers, of sole leather, composing leather heel of shoe.

high shoe. Shoe with upper extending above ankle; often fastened at front with laces, or at side-front with buttons.

hooded heel. Heel covered all in one piece with the back of the shoe, without seam or interruption in line. Same piece continues on over instep to serve as fastening.

ice cube heel. Low, square-cut heel of clear Lucite introduced in 1970. It appeared to be the shape and size of an ice cube.

Child's brown leather **high shoes** with laces. $65-85.

Rubber **heels** from the 1950s.

243

insulated boot. Any boot with a lining for protection against cold, rain, snow, and bad weather. May be lined with fur, acrylic pile, wool, or foam-bonded fabric.

Indian moccasin. True heel-less moccasin in which the sole is made of leather and comes up to form the quarter and part of the vamp of the shoe. Made by Americans in same style since colonial times. Hard soles, sometimes of rubber, are added to produce a more durable shoe than the soft Indian moccasin, generally called **moccasins.**

Insole. Inside of shoe on which the sole of foot rests; usually covered by sock lining, inner or inside sole of shoe, to which upper is stitched and outside sole attached; separate strip as of leather or felt, placed inside the shoe for comfort in walking.

instep. Part of shoe, stocking, or last which covers upper from part of the arch of the foot from ankle to where it joins toes.

jellies. Molded footwear of soft plastic or rubber made in many styles—wedgies, multi-strapped sandals, flat-heeled thongs, high-heeled pumps, and booties. Named for soft, translucent look of jelly in jellybean colors.

Juliet. Women's house slipper with high front and back and goring at U-shaped sides.

klompen. Heavy wooden shoes worn by Dutch; a type of sabot.

last. Wooden form or mold, sometimes reinforced with metal, used in shoe construction to give a shoe its shape. Made on standard measurements taken at ball, waist, and instep of foot. Usually designated only by number.

Infant's boot **last**, 3-1/2-inches long. $65-75.

Wooden shoe **lasts**.

leisure shoe. Any shoe designed for comfortable wear for informal occasions.

loafer. Moccasin-type slip-on shoe, constructed with a slotted strap stitched to the vamp. Also called **penny loafer**, and **chain loafer.** Introduced first for wear by college girls in the 1940s, now classics style.

Louis XV heel. Heel about 1-1/2-inches high, sometimes more, having curved outline, flared as base, placed slightly forward under foot. Popular during reign of Louis XV. Revived as a fashion many times since then.

low. Shoe that ends below ankle. Usually called low-cut.

Lucite. Trademark of E.I. du Pont de Nemours and Company for transparent acrylic plastic material used for handbags, sandals, shoe heels, and jewelry.

majorette boot. Calf-high white boot worn by majorette or cheerleader at athletic events since the 1940s. Some have long white tassel attached to front.

Mamma shoe. Retail store and trade name for shoes worn by older women who stress comfort rather than style. Usually made in a oxford style with medium-high broad heel. Also called **Granny shoe.**

Mary Jane. Low-heeled slipper made of patent leather with a blunt toe, and a single strap over the instep, buttoned or buckled at center or side. A trademarked shoe for children popular since the early 20th century. Named for shoes worn by character Mary Jane in comic strip "Buster Brown" drawn by R. F. Outcault in the early 1900s.

McKay. Shoe made by sole-stitching method invented by Lyman Blake. Similar to welt shoe construction, except that outsole, insole, and upper are all stitched together at one time. So called for Gordon McKay who purchased patent rights. Often called Blake.

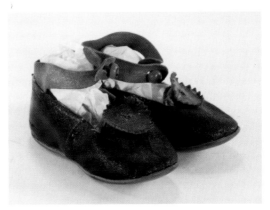

Infant's **Mary Janes**, only 2-inches long. $85-95.

Sample **Mary Janes** from 1910, with the original ordering information. $85-95.

military heel. Heel similar to Cuban, but straighter, heavier, and not so high.

Miranda pump. Platform pump with a high, heavy, flared heel worn in 1969. Named after Carmen Miranda, a popular movie star of the late 1930s and 1940s.

mod boot. Various types of boots worn in mid-1960s in imitation of English mod fashions, for example, the **Beatle boot.**

monk shoe. Closed shoe with wide buckled strap over tongue at instep rather than lacing. Popular for women during the 1940s, and for men during World War II when this style was favored by U.S. Army Air Corps officers. Revived in late 1960s and early 1970s.

monster shoe. Clumsy, bulky shoe with wide bulbous toe and large clunky heel popularized in 1968.

mousers. Women's leather stocking-pants reaching to the waist with attached chunky-type shoes made of shiny wet-look leather. Introduced by Mary Quant, British designer, in 1969.

muk-luk. Originally, Alaskan Eskimo or Indian boot of seal or other animal hides with fur inside. Adapted for military wear in cold climates and for sports or lounging shoes of soft moccasin type.

mule. Women's boudoir slipper having high heel but no quarter and sometimes strap at back. Usually made of satin, fine kid, etc.

nail. Open-toed, flat, heel-less Arabian sandal.

open-back shoe. Shoe with part of upper at heel cut away to expose the heel of the foot. (same as **slingback** shoe)

open-toed shoe. Women's shoe with front of upper cut out to show toes. Popular in the 1920s, 1940s, mid-1970s, and 1980s.

open shank shoe. Women's shoe with closed toe and heel portions but open on sides down to the sole, sometimes with side straps connecting vamp and quarter.

opera pump. Plain, undecorated women's pump with medium to high heel. Upper is cut from a single piece of leather or fabric. Introduced in 1920s and a basic style during the 1940s and 1950s, revived in 1970s.

overshoe. Shoe of rubber or waterproof fabric worn over ordinary footwear as protection against weather; **galosh.**

oxford. Low-cut shoe, ending at instep or lower, usually with three or more eyelets, laced and tied across the instep. May also be strapped or buttoned and have any form of vamp or ornamentation. First used in England more than 300 years ago.

pants boot. Ankle-high shoe boot designed to wear with pants.

penny loafer. Loafer with a slot in the strap across each vamp into which a coin is sometimes inserted. Pennies were originally worn, and were thought to bring good luck.

pinafore heel. Nearly flat heel curving into very low arch. Used on children's shoes.

platform shoe. Shoe with thick mid-sole, usually made of cork and covered so that the wearer appears taller. Popular for women in 1940s and revived by Paris designer, Yves Saint Laurent in 1960s. Worn by men in 1970s. Revived again in the mid-1990s.

play shoe. Any type of shoe for informal wear for beach, lounging, resort, including sandal types, moccasin styles, espadrilles.

pump. Slip-on shoe with low-cut, rounded, or V-shaped throat, usually a medium to high heel sometimes covered with the same material as the upper. Toes vary from rounded to pointed with current style. Sometimes made with open-toe and/or open heel in slingback style. A classic style for women for day or evening since 1920s.

pyramid heel. Medium-high heel with squared base flaring toward the sole—like an inverted pyramid.

quarter. Back part of shoe upper, covering heel, and joined to vamp.

riding boot. High boot coming to below the knee made of high quality leather, usually custom ordered to fit leg. Worn with breeches for horseback riding. May have bootstraps at top for ease in dressing.

roller skate. Above-the-ankle boot made with polyurethane wheels, rubber toe stop, closed with eyelets and speed lacing. Worn for roller skating.

Ruby Keeler shoe. Low-heeled pump tied across instep with ribbon bow similar to tap shoes. Popular for teenagers in early 1970s. Named after tap dancer, Ruby Keeler, popular star of 1930s films, who made a stage comeback on Broadway in 1971 in a revival of the 1917 musical, *No, No, Nanette.*

running. Soft leather shoe having spiked sole. Used by athletes.

sabot. Wooden shoe, sometimes carved in one piece. Worn by French, French Canadians, and other peasants. In recent usage, heavy, wooden-soled shoe with flexible shank. Also called **klompen.**

sabot-strap shoe. Women's shoe with a wide strap across instep usually buckling to one side. May be used on a spectator pump type of shoe.

sandals. Open-type shoes usually held on foot by means of straps. This is a separate category of footwear, distinguished from **shoes, boots, and slippers.**

sculptured heel. Broad medium-high heel made with see-through center introduced in 1960s. Similar to some free-form pieces of sculpture. Used on some wooden clogs in the late 1970s.

seamless. Shoe with a whole vamp, stitched only at the back.

shank. Narrow part of the sole of a shoe beneath instep, or between heel and ball of foot. Sometimes stiffened by a metal piece called a **shank-piece.**

shoe. Foot-covering, having sole, heel, upper (no higher than the ankle), and some means of fastening. Distinguished from the boot by height, and the sandal and slipper by fastening. Parts of the shoe include counter, heel, quarter, shank, sole, upper, and vamp.

shoe buckle. Buckle serving as ornament or fastening of shoe.

shoe button. Button used to fasten shoe.

shoe-lace. Same as **shoestring** or shoe-tie, lace, ribbon, or string for fastening shoe.

shoe-tree. Device used inside shoe or boot to keep it in shape.

shoe stretcher. Form or device placed in shoe when not being worn to help retain its shape; may be wood, plastic, or metal.

side-gore shoe. Slip-on shoe, usually with high vamp, which has triangular insertions of elastic at sides.

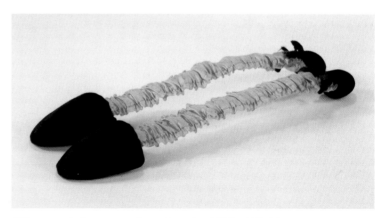

Silk covered **shoe stretchers** from the 1920s. $12-14.

Wood **shoe stretchers** from the
1920s. $20-25.

Shoe stretchers from the
1930s.$10-12.

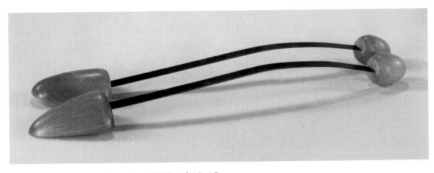

Shoe stretchers from the 1930s. $10-12.

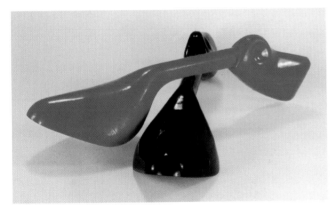

Shoe stretchers from the 1940s. $10-12.

skimmer. Very low cut pump for women with shallow sides, set on low or flat heels, usually made of very soft leather. Also called **shell.**

slide. Toeless open-back sandal with wedgie sole of various heights or a regular heel in all heights which can be made of wood or leather.

slingback. Any shoe with an open back and a strap around the heel of the foot to hold it in place. May be made in pump or sandal style.

sling pump. Women's pump cut away at heel and held in place by a strap around heel.

slipper. Properly any footwear lower than the ankle (excluding rubbers); usually without means of fastening, being merely slipped on the foot.

sole. Bottom part of the shoe under the foot, usually consisting of three parts—out-sole, mid-sole, and innersole or insole.

A leather child's shoe, with a wood **sole**, worn for play during the 1860s. *Courtesy of Donna Sigler.*

Spanish heel. High covered wooden heel, similar to French, but having straight breast and broader base.

spike heel. High heel, higher than French or Spanish, narrow at bottom.

spool heel. Heel having wide horizontal corrugations, giving effect like that of old fashioned spool furniture.

square heel. Heel squared off at back so that it has four corners. Sometimes used with squared effect at toe also.

squaw boot. Below-the-knee boot made of buckskin with fringed turned-down cuff at top, soft sole, and no heel. Originally worn by North American Indian women, it became a fashion item in late 1960s.

stacked heel. Heel built up of horizontal layers of leather. Also called **built-up heel.**

step-in. Shoe with no obvious method of fastening, usually held on snugly by an elastic gore.

stiletto heel. Set-back heel which ends in tiny rounded base, usually fitted with a metal cap. As the walking surface is small, there is an enormous amount of weight on the heel. Used mainly from 1950s to mid-1960s. (Based on small, pointed instrument, *stiletto*, made of ivory, bone, or other hard material, and used in eyelet work for puncturing holes in material).

stockings. Knitted item of wearing apparel covering the foot and leg. Also called hose or hosiery.

Rayon **stockings** from the 1930s. $15-20 per pair.

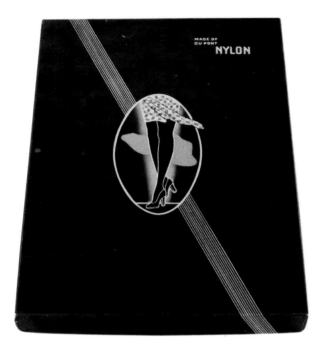

A **stocking** box from the 1940s. $15-18.

A package of nylon **stockings** from the 1950s. $12-14.

A designer **stocking** box from the 1960s. $10-12.

A package of nylon **stockings**
from the 1960s. $10-12.

stocking boot. Fashion boot made of stretch vinyl, leather, or fabric with no zipper fitting the leg closely like a stocking. Sometimes reaches to thigh with attached panties in late 1960s. Also called **body boot.**

straight shoe. The left and right soles are indistinguishable; the soles are "straight" and fitted either foot.

street. Shoe usually of low cut and solid construction, suitable for street wear in town. Distinguished from delicate and sports types.

T-strap. Type of shoe strap running from the center of vamp throat to join ankle strap.

toe pillow. Same as toe stretcher.

Velvet **toe pillows** from the 1920s. $12-15.

Toe pillows from the 1920s. $12-14.

Toe pillows from the 1930s. $10-12.

toe stretcher. Similar to shoe stretcher, placed in toe of shoe when not being worn to retain toe of shoe's shape.

upper. Part of shoe above sole and heel, consisting of vamp, quarter, counter, and lining.

vamp. Part of shoe upper over toe and instep.

walking shoe. Any comfortable shoe with a relatively low heel, sometimes made with a cushion or crepe sole, worn more for comfort than style.

wedge heel. Heel raised by a wedge-shaped piece between flat sole and body of shoe.

wedge-soled. Having a wedge-shaped piece making a solid sole, flat on ground from heel to toe. Term applied to certain style of shoe.

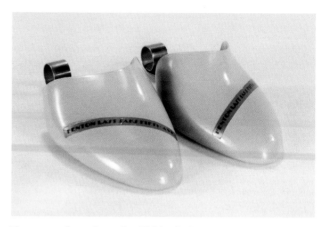

Toe stretchers from the 1930s. $12-14.

Toe stretchers from the 1930s. $10-12.

wedgies. Shoes with wedge-shaped heels completely joined to soles under the arches, made in all styles and heel heights. Popular for women in the late 1940s, revived for women and also worn by men in the 1970s. Originally made with high wedge, now made with low-and-medium wedges.

Woolworth shoe. Shoe which has been sold in millions of Woolworth stores (department store no longer in business; started as "5 & 10"). Made of cotton canvas, in sandal style, in red, navy, paisley, black, or white. This shoe has sold for more than 50 years and has been entered in the permanent collection of the Metropolitan Museum of Art Costume Collection. Also called **landlady shoe**.

Index

Author's note: Names of manufacturers, retailers, and designers are recorded as they are printed on the insoles of the shoes, which accounts for the somewhat unusual use of capital and lower case letters in descriptive material and in the corresponding index entries.